Daily Life in Johnson's London

Daily Life in Johnson's London

Richard B. Schwartz

The University of Wisconsin Press

Published by

The University of Wisconsin Press
114 North Murray Street
Madison, Wisconsin 53715

The University of Wisconsin Press, Ltd.
1 Gower Street
London WC1E 6HA, England

Printings 1983, 1985

Printed in the United States of America

Library of Congress Cataloging in Publication Data

Schwartz, Richard B.
  Daily life in Johnson's London.
  Bibliography: pp. 181–190.
  Includes index.
    1. London (England)—Social life and customs—18th
century. 2. London (England)—Description—to 1800.
3. Johnson, Samuel, 1709–1784—Homes and haunts—
England—London. I. Title.
DA682.S38   1983   942.107   83-50080
ISBN 0-299-09490-1
ISBN 0-299-09494-4 (pbk.)

for Judith and Jonathan

Contents

Acknowledgments

The preparation of this book has been supported by a fellowship from the American Council of Learned Societies and an H. I. Romnes Fellowship awarded by the University of Wisconsin, Madison. A part of Chapter IV appeared in different form in *The Unknown Samuel Johnson,* ed. John J. Burke and Donald Kay (University of Wisconsin Press, 1982). I am grateful to a number of colleagues for their advice and encouragement along the way: John Abbott, Percy Adams, Paul Alkon, Martine Brownley, Vincent Carretta, the late James Clifford, Thomas Curley, Jean Hagstrum, Mary Hyde, Donald Greene, Frank McConnell, Maximilian Novak, Albrecht Strauss, and Clarence Tracy. Patricia A. Hansen and Jamea French read the book in manuscript and made helpful suggestions. Joseph Jeffs, Mark Cohen, and especially David Hagen of the Georgetown University Library provided invaluable help with the illustrations. Georgette Dorn of the Library of Congress provided timely help in the final stages of the project. My principal debt is to my wife, Judith, and son, Jonathan, who would have made life in the eighteenth century a pleasure and who make life in the twentieth a joy.

Wolf Trap
Ayr Hill, Virginia
September 1982

Introduction

This book has been written with several purposes in mind. It is intended to be an introduction to certain aspects of eighteenth-century social history, elements of life and experience which constitute the setting for much eighteenth-century literature. I have tried to assemble that material which would be of greatest interest to the general reader and, at the same time, most pertinent for the student of eighteenth-century literature. Although this book has not been written for scholars, it is not without a scholarly dimension. One of the issues confronting Johnson's modern biographers is the amount of attention which should be devoted to the details of his daily life. Boswell could take much for granted that we cannot. Matters and experiences with which Boswell's audience were familiar must be resuscitated for the modern reader. Moreover, given his love of Johnson and his love of London, Boswell sometimes presented his subject and his setting in ways which, though faithful to Boswell's own values and perceptions, tended to romanticize London and its famous denizen. My purpose is not to provide an "alternative" to Boswell but rather to sketch in some of the details which he very properly omits and to try to provide a portion of the context in which his biography and Johnson's experience may best be understood.

The book treats *Johnson's* London, but it looks forward and backward and is not restricted to the London of 1737–84. Johnson is an inseparable part of eighteenth-century London —for many its most famous citizen and most frequently quoted defender—but the city could be seen from the point of view of many other inhabitants. Johnson, however, was there at a time of important change. He nearly spans the century and combines a love of the past, of history, and of tradition, with a keen and youthful eye on the future. Moreover, his personal experience, as I will argue later, spans several separate spheres of social activity in a way which is unique. He knows the worlds of the titled, the grand, the great, the rich, the squierarchy, the middle class, the industrious and not-so-industrious poor, the desperate, and all the gradations between them. He knows the world of the professions: of medicine, law, the schools, and the church; he knows the world of trade and the world of politics. He lived in or near the city for nearly fifty of his adult years. Though he is associated with Fleet Street and its immediate environs, his experience was certainly not limited to those sections of the metropolis. There are two other reasons for considering *his* London. First, his life is of such broad human interest and common human concern—W. J. Bate has termed it a "life of allegory"—that further understanding of that life is always welcome because it is always instructive. Second, Johnson's thought on any subject commands our attention, and his thoughts on many subjects have come to command our assent. London is one of his favorite subjects, and his comments on it are best understood in the context of daily London life. For example, his comments on the importance of "subordination" are best seen in the framework in which they were offered, in a society with virtually no police force, a society in which controls on one's actions come from within more often than from without. It is hoped that this study will aid in the clarification of certain areas of Johnson's thought.

Johnson's experience informs this study, but it does not dominate it. I have tried to see the city as he would have seen it and stress those details in which he would have been interested. He does not stand in the foreground of each chapter—this is not a partial biography—but I have considered him to be a particularly useful, albeit sometimes silent, guide. He is an especially appropriate figure for this purpose, for the daily vicissitudes of life are not only favorite Johnsonian subjects but subjects whose importance he defends in detail. He once wrote to Giuseppe Baretti that "a mind able to see common incidents in their real state, is disposed by very common incidents to very serious contemplations" (*Letters,* 1:140). In his monumental study of the family, sex, and marriage from the Renaissance to the nineteenth century, Lawrence Stone begins with a quotation from Johnson's eighty-fourth *Idler* on the importance of what Johnson terms "the general surface of life." Johnson's remarks are among the most noteworthy anticipations of the growing twentieth-century interest in social history. One of the most important of these comments occurs in his *Journey to the Western Islands of Scotland*; he is apologizing for his "diminutive observations" on Scottish windows:

> But it must be remembered, that life consists not of a series of illustrious actions, or elegant enjoyments; the greater part of our time passes in compliance with necessities, in the performance of daily duties, in the removal of small inconveniencies, in the procurement of petty pleasures; and we are well or ill at ease, as the main stream of life glides on smoothly, or is ruffled by small obstacles and frequent interruption. The true state of every nation is the state of common life. . . . The great mass of nations is neither rich nor gay: they whose aggregate constitutes the people, are found in the streets, and the villages, in the shops and farms; and from them collectively considered, must the measure of general prosperity be taken. [P. 22]

The "diminutive observations" are, in fact, the basis upon which Johnson's wisdom was built. Boswell comments that Johnson's judgments carry conviction because "they are founded on . . . common sense, and a very attentive and minute survey of real life" (*Life*, 4:428). Johnson once projected the writing of a work to be entitled "Considerations upon the present state of London" (*Life*, 4:382n). Such a work would have been informed both by his intimate knowledge of the city and by his fascination with the city's ways, but it was never written. One of its strengths might well have been the balance of its presentation, for Johnson's remarks on London indicate his awareness of the city's contrasts and extremes, a matter which it is curiously easy to forget.

In act 4 of Wycherley's *Country Wife* (1675), Lucy comments that "the country is as terrible, I find, to our young English ladies, as a monastery to those abroad; and, on my virginity, I think they would rather marry a London jailer than a high sheriff of a county, since neither can stir from his employment. Formerly women of wit married fools for a great estate, a fine seat, or the like; but now 'tis for a pretty seat in Lincoln's Inn Fields, St. James's Fields, or the Pall Mall." Like so many of the plays of the period this one is set in London, not in the London of poverty or crime but in the London of the theatre world, the Covent Garden London in which the play acting, masking, and wit of the theatre is mirrored in "real" life, the London of wealth, style, and fashion in which the middle class seldom intrudes and in which the beggar has no place at all. The theatre has always had a special effect on our sense of setting, even though we are aware of the illusion which it creates, for it is an illusion which is a source of great comfort. Restoration comedy, for example, excludes many aspects of common life and focuses upon the problems and concerns of a statistically inconsequential percentage of the population. The actions and conflicts of these characters are, however, extremely important to us, for they create a world of wit, intrigue, innuendo, and double entendre, a world of sparks, bloods, and fops, of ladies of fashion, of easy and uneasy virtue, and of rakes, jealous husbands, pretenders to learning, and bumpkins at the mercy of Londoners, a world which is the "Restoration."

This "Restoration" is an intellectual construct, not a historical period, for it tends to exclude fires, plagues, wars, cabals, bloodless revolutions, popish plots, rebellions, urban poverty, disease, trade (to a great extent), and such seemingly mundane though historically consequential events as the development of the British civil service. It may cast a glance at contemporary life—at science, for example—but often to hold such things up to ridicule, for one of the pleasures of the "Restoration" is its tendency to exclude, a process which may cause pain but also a process which systematically keeps certain types of pain at a distance. A modern dramatic analogue would be the thriller or murder mystery, playing to our illusions of England as a country of gardens and stately homes, with "character" personalities capable of crime and violence but in possession of the traditional virtues and propensities which will ensure a proper resolution of the conflict and solving of the crime as well as a large portion of cleverness and fun in the meantime. This is an England from which such issues as inflation, labor unrest, the price of Middle Eastern oil, and Middle Eastern speculation in West End real estate are excluded, while our attention fixes upon the far more genial world of sherry, woolens, roses, thatched cottages, walking sticks, drafty halls, and police constables. This type of play, involving a process of exclusion, provides what Johnson would term harmless entertainment, that is, entertainment which does not do us physical or moral harm. It is not trivial; its importance to continuing, large audiences commands our attention as it would have commanded Johnson's. It is a part of cultural and intellectual history and, as such, deserves study. It is not, however, a reliable introduction to the pattern of twentieth-century English society, just as a Restoration comedy is not a particularly useful entrée into the complex world of late-seventeenth-century London.

Nevertheless, selectivity and exclusion are necessities for both the writer and the painter. The problem for modern students of eighteenth-century life and literature is that certain writers and painters were so effective in this regard. The England and, for our purposes, the London of the eighteenth century come down to us in forms which initially appear to be contradictory. The periodical essays of Addison and Steele, for example, which are designed to exclude the types of crimes for which one will be sent to hell or to prison, evoke an eighteenth century of fashion, foible, and middle-class intellectual development, of cosmetics, hoop petticoats, political obsessiveness, and clubableness, of squires, tradesmen, and members of the professions, of servants, chaplains, widows, and wits, of the world of the theatre, the internal world of Locke, the external world of Newton, the beauty of the spacious firmament on high and the soul-stirring appeal of the Royal Exchange. There are Mohocks (contemporary street toughs), atheists, and other intruders in this world, but not enough of them to counterbalance the image of clubs, coffee and chocolate houses, of snuff, perukes, tea, and clay pipes.

The world of Hogarth, on the other hand, is a quite different matter. There we find disease and violence, filth, noise, falling buildings and falling people, chaos, poverty, distress, disarray, infidelity, drunkenness, suicide, betrayal, and insanity, the world of the brothel, the prison, the mob, and the street. This, of course, is only a part of Hogarth's work. Just as Addison and Steele know suffering, sin, and crime, and the worlds beyond the immediate concerns of the middle class, Hogarth knows virtue, beauty, order, and humanity. The point is that these men produced works in which certain aspects of experience are so effectively realized that they may displace others. Civility or brutality can eclipse the other, and we can embrace an artistic construct as a faithful representation of life as lived within a historical period.

The best way to enter the world of eighteenth-century London is to keep both the civility and brutality in mind, for the most striking characteristics of the period are its contrasts and extremes. Archenholz described the eighteenth-century England which he found as a place "where every thing is in extremes" (*A Picture of England,* p. 115). E. B. Chancellor writes that "every period has its essential characteristic. That of the 18th century is . . . contrast" (*The Eighteenth Century in London,* p. 46). Dorothy George comments that "we can regard the eighteenth century as an age of corruption, oligarchy, privilege, materialism, or we can regard it as an age of common sense, good humour, reasonableness, and toleration—one view does not exclude the other" (*England in Transition,* p. 65).

Johnson was attracted to London because of, among other things, its variety, extent, and wealth of intellectual entertainment. His friend Elizabeth Carter described the country as a region "of obscurity and uninterrupted dullness, where nothing remarkable ever happened since the landing of Julius Caesar and all that passes ten miles distant is as absolutely unknown as if it fell out in the country of Prester John." One tires of London only when one tires of life.

Boswell's London, a city of rich literary and social associations, is seen in quasi-religious terms, with Johnson's residences and haunts as quasi-shrines. Boswell speaks of his own reverence and devotion when he discusses them. It is well to keep such positive responses in mind, for it will often seem, in the pages that follow, that the unpleasant has supplanted the pleasant, that horrors are being enumerated to the exclusion of delights. Two things should be kept in mind. First, London attracted many who were not forced to reside there through economic necessity. In other words, even if it was smoky, malodorous, and disease-ridden, contemporaries were drawn to it in numbers. Its attractions were many. Second, though the state of the capital provoked both public and parliamentary complaints, much was taken for granted that we would find intolerable. A social historian of the twenty-second century might well chronicle the absurdities, outrages, unconquered diseases, and primitive transportation of the twentieth century for an audience looking on our times with disgust and disbelief. Yet while we complain of certain aspects of our own experience there are few who consider us hopelessly backward, primitive, and benighted. We accept things and tolerate circumstances just as the eighteenth century did, and it is possible that in the case of technological advance and amelioration of daily ills, hindsight can be more painful than the immediate experience of the situations which have been remedied.

Nevertheless, we should not gloss over the distance between the eighteenth century and the twentieth, for the advances in certain areas—medicine and sanitation, for example—have been enormous, and we can properly wonder how Johnson's contemporaries survived the circumstances in which they lived. At times we think of the eighteenth century in the terms presented by late-nineteenth-century historians, a time of balance, good sense, and the successful search for the middle way between conflicting extremes. In point of fact, the period considered balance and sense normative because it so seldom found them in practice.

This is a time when a soldier fought for sixpence a day while hundreds of pounds were bet on the mains at the Whitehall cockpit, when a laborer might earn ten shillings a week and a lord lose tens of thousands of pounds at hazard in an evening, when a man might own hand-tooled and enameled snuffboxes for every night of the week but bathe only twice a year, when ladies purchased ivory-handled back scratchers—to counterattack against the vermin with which they were infested, a time when a man might fight a duel to the death over the pronunciation of Greek, a time when some children sat to Reynolds and others had their teeth forcibly extracted to be sold to the toothless wealthy.

Such extremes were not always experienced. The Thames waterman did not dine with the nobility, just as the nobility stayed clear of the criminal dens in the section adjacent to the Temple known as Alsatia, but many did experience the contrasts which the age presented, particularly the literary men, who, at different times in their lives, moved in quite different circles. In this regard few shared the breadth of experience and the depth of interest, curiosity, and compassion of Johnson. When he comments on London he speaks of a London in all its complexity—the vital and the morbid, the gay and the hopelessly depressed—and that, as Boswell says, is why his judgments carry conviction.

Needless to say, I have not attempted to capture all of that complexity in this book. What I have tried to do is bring together those primary and secondary materials which, in combination, give the modern reader a sense of the texture of daily life in the eighteenth century. There are many specialized studies listed in the bibliography to which the interested reader should turn for further information on specific topics. I have not tried to supersede such studies, but rather, to gather from such materials those facts and details which are particularly useful for a reader attempting to achieve a sense of life as lived within this period. I have also relied heavily on contemporary travelers' accounts. Eighteenth-century foreigners discovering London are useful guides for their twentieth-century counterparts, particularly when they are struck by repeating aspects of life and repeating patterns of behavior. My hope is that readers of this book will be able to develop a set of mental images of the eighteenth century which will enable them to approach the history and literature of the period with greater appreciation for those details of life which often go unmentioned or unnoticed.

Daily Life in
Johnson's London

I. Sights, Sounds, and Smells

When the skyline of eighteenth-century London was not enveloped in the smoke from sea-coal fires, certain still-familiar structures were visible: the Abbey, the Tower, the dome of St. Paul's, and Wren's memorial of the great fire, the Monument. But there were striking differences. Chief among them was the predominance of church steeples, which were not yet dwarfed or concealed by modern buildings. London is a city of churches. By the later eighteenth century there were over three hundred of them. Approximately half were Anglican parish churches and chapels. There were three Jewish synagogues and nearly twenty Catholic chapels. There were churches, chapels, and meetinghouses for French Protestants, for the Germans, the Dutch, and the Danes, for Independents, Presbyterians, Baptists, and Quakers. "This is the country of sects," Voltaire proclaimed; "an Englishman, as a free man, goes to Heaven by whatever road he pleases" (*Philosophical Letters*, p. 22).

The skyline was also notable in the number of its high, round chimneys, standing amidst the steeples of its churches. Beneath the smoke issuing from them were over a dozen hospitals, several colleges, over two dozen public prisons, dozens of schools and charity schools, some forty markets, fifteen inns of court, as well as fairs, artillery grounds, pesthouses, royal palaces, and bishops' palaces. The city's width from Hyde Park corner to Limehouse was about five miles, its north-south measure, some two to three miles depending on the points of measurement.

Victoria Embankment was not yet built, and the Thames of the eighteenth century was both wider and more shallow than its modern counterpart. When it froze, frost fairs were held

London at mid-century, its skyline dominated by church spires. High-masted ships remain below London Bridge.

upon it. The river was dense with vessels, particularly below London Bridge. By the latter part of the century new bridges disposed of the need for the old horse-ferry at Westminster. Traffic upon the Thames was slow and sometimes perilous. The smell of sewage was apparent even though the river remained the city's chief source for its supply of water. The city's streets were covered with hackney coaches (nearly a thousand of them) and sedan chairs, as well as innumerable carts and wagons. The wooden houses swept away by the great fire had been replaced with structures of brick and stone, structures which would inhibit both the spread of flames and the gnawing of flea-infested, potentially plague-carrying rats.

The streets were filled with people. Their numbers, however, are difficult to estimate. Although an official census had been proposed as early as 1753, it was not finally taken until 1801. At that time, allowing for a certain level of nonresident population, London had 900,000 of the country's nearly 10 million people. As a rough rule of thumb, the greater London of Johnson's time contained approximately one-tenth of the total population and over half of the country's urban population. Prior to the census the chief sources of statistics are parish registers and bills of mortality, but the records are ecclesiastical rather than civil. They register baptisms, not births, and interments rather than deaths. Individual record-keeping was very uneven. The Jews and Catholics had their own burial grounds; the Jews and Quakers were not christened and Catholic christenings were not registered, so the statistics are unreliable, particularly for the city of London with its mixed population, multiple faiths, travelers, itinerant wealthy, and large number of disconnected, drifting poor. Dorothy George's estimate would place the city's population at approximately 675,000 at the beginning of the eighteenth century, with the figure increasing markedly by the beginning of the nineteenth (*London Life in the Eighteenth Century,* p. 329). Some estimate it to be lower at the beginning of the century—at, for example, 500,000—but estimates are perforce rough. The Birmingham to which the young Johnson walked was perhaps a city of 20,000–25,000, probably larger than Hull, Sheffield, Nottingham, or Leeds, but smaller than Bristol, Norwich, Manchester, or Liverpool.

The concentration of activity in the city of London is striking. It is the center of government, of trade, of entertainment, of communications, of finance, of intellectual life, and of fashion. Educationally, Oxford and Cambridge are each but fifty miles away. The city serves functions which, in the United States for example, are divided among such cities as Boston, Los Angeles, Chicago, Washington, and New York. All were concentrated in eighteenth-century London, a city comparable in its population to modern Edinburgh, or in the United States to Cincinnati or Milwaukee. The combination of concentration of activity and comparative smallness of population is worth remarking. The pattern of life and intellectual interchange which resulted from this circumstance is significant, particularly for students of literature.

For example, the literary traditions in which a writer in the eighteenth century found himself were coupled with neighborhood traditions and associations. Being near St. Bride's Church and having lived in Fetter Lane, Johnson was close to the ghosts of Milton and Dryden. When he celebrated Charlotte Lennox's literary activities, it was at a tavern once frequented by Ben Jonson. Contemporary writers often lived in close proximity to one another and in close proximity to their publishers. One of the reasons Johnson rented the Gough Square residence was the fact that it was near his printer, Strahan, in New Street Square.

The close working relationship between eighteenth-century writer and eighteenth-century bookseller is well known, partly because of Johnson's comments which Boswell has recorded for us. A question not often addressed but one that is particularly appropriate concerns the relation between literary theory and literary practice within the context of a closely knit community. In our own time literary critics and theorists live in a separate world from literary artists. Moreover, they are separated geographically and communicate, if at all, largely through print. In Johnson's London theorists and practitioners were often close friends or bitter personal enemies. Scholars like Edmond Malone or Bishop Percy were close friends of professional writers. In the case of Malone and Boswell, the scholar played an active role in the work of the writer. If one remembers that perhaps 75 percent of London's population consisted of the faceless poor, we have a literary and intellectual environment which is very small and often interlaced. We can expect literary relationships and literary influence of a much different nature from those which we know today.

Of course there are other pertinent relationships as well. Literary figures might serve directly in the government, as Addison did, or serve as government apologists in the popular press. There was, in many cases, proximity to the monarch (Johnson and Boswell both meeting the king; Arbuthnot serving as Queen Anne's physician-in-ordinary) or personal proximity to power and influence (Boswell cavorting on the Continent with Bute's son, Lord Mountstuart). Literary figures might participate directly in the world of business and trade, as Defoe and Richardson did, or through personal con-

The Strand and St. Clement Danes. Note the shop signs, and the posts separating the pedestrian walkways.

nections, as Johnson did with the Southwark brewer Henry Thrale. There were close ties with the world of art and of music, with the world of medicine, of law, and of science. The differences in interests, inclinations, and attitudes between eighteenth- and twentieth-century writers, like the differences in their relations with their publishers, their audiences, and their governments, can be exaggerated easily. Nonetheless, the physical and social circumstances in which the eighteenth-century writer found himself should not be forgotten or over-looked. His ties with the separate segments of his society and the separate areas of intellectual and artistic activity were much closer than they usually are today, and the impact of that situation on literary practice and personal interests could be considerable. Many now would judge that situation to be a comparatively salutary one.

If eighteenth-century London offered writers a stimulating intellectual atmosphere, its physical circumstances were far less appealing. The day-to-day state of the capital was, by modern standards, appalling. One factor, which we may forget, for example, is the function of horses in eighteenth-century travel. London was filled with horses and the smells and waste materials associated with them. The streets were nearly always covered with mire. One sometimes sees houses constructed with high steps so that the wealthy residents could step into a carriage from the steps without entering the muck below. Here is Grosley, commenting on the section of the Strand to which Johnson would go to worship:

> In the most beautiful part of the Strand and near St. Clement's Church, I have, during my whole stay in London, seen the middle of the street constantly foul with a dirty puddle to the height of three or four inches; a puddle where splashings cover those who walk on foot, fill coaches when their windows happen not to be up, and bedawb all the lower parts of such houses as are exposed to it. In consequence of this, the prentices are frequently employed in washing the fronts of their houses, in order to take off the daubings of dirt which they had contracted over night. [*A Tour to London*, 1:33–34]

Gay (*Trivia*, l. 25) writes of the "miry Sides" of coaches and offers particular advice on the purchase of shoes. He recommends firm, well-hammered soles and cautions buyers to make certain that their shoes fit properly. This was to prevent the turning of ankles on street stones and to help guard against the accumulated muck through which one had to walk. Along with the dirt, dust, and animal manure, there was the addition of London rain and drizzle and animal and human urine.

The city's water supply system also contributed to the problem, for the water was pumped through hollowed tree trunks (generally of elm) beneath London streets. These trunks were joined with iron unions. The seal was not tight, and the normal deterioration of the wood resulted in a seepage rate of approximately 25 percent. The bore of the mains was usually about six inches; their effective life was about four years. The clay soil

Boring the water mains.

minimized the spread of the leakage for a time, however, so that full replacement generally came after about twenty years. When one of these mains burst, the city streets had sudden springs. Thus, the presence of slime and odoriferous mud was well nigh constant. Dust, however, was not really a welcome alternative. When the streets were dry, they were watered by water carts which carried barrels or casks pierced with holes.

The filth of the streets was carried off, to some extent, by kennels (in the middle of the street, very often, and sometimes containing dead cats), but much of the muck was either redistributed or washed into the Thames, a major thoroughfare for merchants and travelers and, as has already been indicated, the principal source of the city's water supply. Some filth stayed in place. The streets would be dotted with pools of urine and stagnant water. Butchers threw their offal into the streets, and one must remember that animals were sometimes slaughtered in private dwellings in densely populated neighborhoods. Dead animals (dogs, cats, rodents, even horses) were left to decay in the streets where they lay. In darker corners of the city an occasional human corpse might also be found. Bacterial infections were constant, a situation exacerbated by the eating of spoiled food.

London street, with open sewer and public water supply.

Some did profit from this situation. For example, a good deal of street dung was collected and taken by barge up river to the market garden land of Pimlico. The dung fertilized the soil and yielded large crops of melons and vegetables. One of the principal pick-up points was at Whitefriars dung wharf. But scouring the city could prove dangerous. In 1749, for example, a body was found in Fleet Ditch. It was reasoned that the individual was probably searching the sewer for dead dogs for the benefit of their skins.

The state of the pavement affected life in other ways as well. The cobbles were subject to movement and damage from carriage wheels. Wider wheels, however, would reduce the need for repairs, for they would ram the stones and keep them in place; thus, carriages with wide wheels were exempt from paying certain duties. Six-inch wheels, however, brought unfortunate side effects. They made the carriages very heavy and the splashing of muck both more frequent and more copious. They were metal, of course, and added considerably to street noise as well as to the discomfort of passengers.

Pedestrians were afforded a bit of protection by the footpaths provided for them. Saussure wrote to his family that "the streets being generally very muddy, the passers-by get terribly bespattered and dirty. Pedestrians, it is true, would be far worse off were there not on either side of the street a sort of elevated footpath for their convenience" (*A Foreign View of England,* p. 167). These footpaths (later to be improved and turned into actual sidewalks) were marked by rows of stone posts—the posts which Johnson nervously touched. Coaches were not permitted on the footpaths, under heavy penalty, and coachmen would sit in traffic snarls literally for hours rather than encroach on the footpaths. Sedan chairs, however, were allowed on the footpaths. A pedestrian would be attentive to such cries as "Have care" or "By your leave, sir," for if he failed to respond, the bearers might, in their hurry, knock him down. Given the number of sounds to which the pedestrian would be subjected it is not unlikely that bearers' cries were frequently inaudible. Sedan chairs would also enter buildings, allowing their passengers to disembark in the halls of their homes.

Prior to the improvement of roads, the wealthy would attempt to enhance their possibility of movement through the streets by sending out running footmen who would precede the coach, attempt to clear the way, and, if possible, impress the passersby with the importance of their masters. They carried white canes; the best of them could run at least seven miles an hour.

The physical obstacles and difficulties impeding travel were compounded by the presence of criminals and ruffians. One bit of protection was afforded by street lighting, an aspect of London life for which foreign travelers had consistent praise.

Saussure, for example, writes of the contrasts in London districts but praises the general consistency of the lighting of the streets: "A number of [the streets] are dirty, narrow, and badly built; others again are wide and straight, bordered with fine houses. Most of the streets are wonderfully well lighted, for in front of each house hangs a lantern or a large globe of glass, inside of which is placed a lamp which burns all night" (*A Foreign View of England*, p. 67). Contemporaries were fond of retelling the story of the German prince who arrived in London with joy, thinking that the streets had been lit for him, an indication of the uncommonness of the extent of the lighting. Archenholz, writing late in the century, saw street lamps which often consisted of two, three, or even four branches. They were enclosed in crystal globes, attached to iron supports, and were lit at sunset. "In Oxford-street alone," he writes, "there are more lamps than in all Paris" (*A Picture of England*, p. 85).

In the early eighteenth century those fronting on streets or courts were responsible for street-lighting on moonless nights from Michaelmas to Lady Day between 6 and 11 P.M. They used tallow candles in horn lanterns. These were replaced by oil lamps. Grosley, touring in 1765, says of the oil lamps that they light the footpaths, but "convey to the middle of the street only a glimmering" (*A Tour to London*, 1:41). Gas lights came to London in 1807.

Despite the advanced state of eighteenth-century London lighting there was still work for the link boys. As the name implies, the links conducted pedestrians through the steets in stages. They carried torches and led the way for anxious travelers. At times the links were in league with footpads and would lead victims into traps. Homes were often equipped with a link extinguisher—long and conical, projecting from buildings in such a way that the link boy could easily insert the torch into it. Some may still be seen today.

Kalm, a member of the Swedish Academy of Sciences who studied with Linnaeus, visited London in 1748. With a specialist's interest in trees and foliage, Kalm noted that the most common tree in London was the elm. There were also many willows, but the elm predominated for a number of reasons: its

Link extinguisher.

usefulness to carpenters, the fact that it keeps its leaves until the autumn, its ability to provide excellent shade, and the fact that it bears up well under the rigors of coal smoke (*Kalm's Account of His Visit to England,* pp. 86–88). Other travelers were more taken with the other aspect of London streets which, with the lighting, was particularly striking: London shop signs.

These brightly painted signs projected from buildings and served two principal purposes: advertising for the potential customer and a "translation" of the tradesman's enterprise and/or locale into pictorial language so that an illiterate coachman could identify the shop. The signs were sometimes huge, thus blocking the passage of air and sunlight (whose ingress and egress were already limited by the government's tax on windows). Some signs came crashing down on pedestrians, and there are accounts of signs pulling down the fronts of buildings to which they were attached. The Westminster Act of 1762 provided that the signs were to be placed flat against the buildings or be removed.

The fact that many lived in close quarters increased the problem of inadequate air and light. Landlords routinely blocked off windows to reduce the paying of tax. The tax on windows was first imposed in 1696. It was repeatedly strengthened and not finally repealed until 1851. The reason is clear. By the mid-nineteenth century the tax was yielding close to £2,000,000 per year. The tax increased with the number of windows, and tenements were assessed as whole houses rather than as sets of separate dwellings. Hence windows were sealed or blocked off, with disastrous results for the inhabitants.

The problem of sanitation was no less severe. Water closets were not seen until the later eighteenth century and then only in the homes of the wealthy, designed by such architects as Robert Adam. Unless one lived over a sewer, the answer was a garden privy or basement cesspit, to be emptied periodically by a night soil man. Sir Joshua Reynolds' outside privy at his home in Leicester Fields is the occasion of a famous anecdote concerning Reynolds' work habits. Reluctant to lose any studio time, Reynolds installed a back staircase leading to the garden privy. When forced to leave his work, Reynolds hastened down the stairs, taking five or six at a time on the way to the privy (Clifford, *Dictionary Johnson*, p. 19).

For those without gardens the cesspit would generally be located in the basement of the dwelling, with chamber pots carried to it from upstairs. An external pit between basement and street would be a nice compromise (Johnson's Gough Square residence may well have been so equipped), for it would remove the need for the night soil man to carry the contents of the cesspit through the house, as well as cut down on the odors in the house between the night soil man's visits. There is no doubt that the sanitation systems and the wells-and-pump water supply systems became intermingled, again with particularly bad results for the poor, dwelling in congested areas and relying on public water supplies.

Londoners who survived were hearty, as Johnson was fond

of pointing out. With regard to sanitation, however, they were not squeamish. Pepys was certainly not alone in his propensity for urinating in the fireplace when chamber pots were unavailable. After a formal dinner the women would routinely retire to close stools in remote sections of the house, while the men remained at table and had pots brought to them. They then used them, in the dining room, with little or no interruption of the offering of successive, seemingly endless, toasts. (Foreigners were particularly struck by the length of time spent in postprandial drinking and toasting.) There are accounts of sideboards stored with chamber pots and of sliding wall panels which were designed to preclude the necessity for the servants to enter the dining room. They could place the pots behind the panels from another room (most likely the kitchen) and receive the filled pots when their masters replaced them behind the panels. The old practice of emptying chamber pots out of windows was associated in the mind of the eighteenth-century Englishman with the practices of the barbarous Scots, but it is doubtful that the practice disappeared in England as quickly as Englishmen would have the Scots believe.

Although eighteenth-century sanitation and hygiene might strike us as coarse, some contemporaries thought that the English, particularly the English ladies, were excessively delicate. Samuel Rolleston writes of a gentleman in Holland in a multi-seat privy who found himself next to a woman who offered him her "muscle shell by way of scraper" after she was finished using it (Clifford, *Dictionary Johnson,* p. 21).

The chief point to keep in mind is that the eighteenth-century Londoner confronted both the sight and smell of waste materials far more frequently and far more directly than his modern counterpart. The point is important, for it is not commonly a part of our mental image of the period. When we think of gentlemen in hand-tailored brocade waistcoats, we think of them dancing minuets, listening to Mozart, or, like Edward Gibbon, tapping snuff boxes. We seldom think of them so dressed and urinating at the table. So too, we talk of such things as Swift's "excremental vision," but we should consider the extent to which we are struck by Swift's talk of excrement in the context of routine eighteenth-century contact with it.

The foreign traveler in the eighteenth century was less troubled by the smell of London privies than by the smell of coal smoke in which he was routinely enveloped, smoke whose particles blackened the snow, homes, statuary, and even the horses. Soot was used as manure; Kalm reports it selling for ten pence a bushel. Coal ash was mixed with clay in order to make stronger brick or tile. At the same time he discussed the usefulness of coal and its by-products, however, Kalm complained of an intense cough during his stay in London. Moritz, describing a morning in London in 1782, writes that "everything in the streets . . . seemed dark even to blackness" (*Journeys of a German in England in 1782,* p. 26). The time was 10 A.M. Kalm reports a fire in 1748 in which over one hundred houses near the Royal Exchange were burned down. Kalm was not even aware of its occurrence until he saw reports of the fire in the newspapers—partly because of the size of the city, but also "partly by the thick and voluminous smoke, which, especially at this time of year [late March], floats over the town" (*Kalm's Account of His Visit to England,* pp. 88–89). Grosley was particularly bothered by the coal smoke. He writes that "if we add to the inconveniency of the dirt, the smoke, which being mixed with a constant fog, covers London, and wraps it up intirely, we shall find in this city, all those particulars which offended Horace most in that of Rome" (*A Tour to London,* 1:43–44).

The smoke came from coal fires in homes (which would, of course, be reduced during the four to five months of warm weather) but also from the fires of tradesmen. There was smoke, for example, from glasshouses, from earthenware factories, from blacksmiths' and gunsmiths' shops, and from dyers' yards. As we follow the buoyant and youthful Boswell through the streets of London it is hard to remember the pall which hung over the city. Grosley writes: "This smoke, being loaded with terrestrial particles, and rolling in a thick, heavy atmosphere, forms a cloud which envelopes London like a mantle; a cloud which the sun pervades but rarely; a cloud which, recoiling back upon itself, suffers the sun to break out only now and then, which casual appearance procures the Londoners a few of what they call *glorious days*" (*A Tour to London*, 1:44). The particles brought "black rains" which kept clothes scourers in business. Grosley speculates that sea-coal fires and their smoke might even be responsible for the melancholy which besets the English, for "the terrestrial and mineral particles . . . insinuate themselves into the blood of those who are always inhaling them, [and] render it dull and heavy, and carry with them new principles of melancholy" (ibid., pp. 166–67).

The smoke was not as great as that of the great fire of 1666, smoke from which was visible in Oxford, but its effects were still dramatic. The smell of the smoke, combined with other city smells such as the stench from the Thames, was such that, with a proper wind, the city could be smelled from several miles away. Archenholz, who writes generally as an anglophile (sometimes nearly as a tourist agent), still must say that "the greatest objection that can be urged against England is the insalubrity of the air, and the indispensable custom of burning coals" (*A Picture of England*, p. 58).

Most modern readers are familiar with the smell of coal smoke. One other notable eighteenth-century smell has, fortunately, become less familiar. London cemeteries contained communal graves, or "poors' holes." These were deep enough for seven tiers of coffins, with three or four coffins to a tier. The pits were left open until they were completely filled, with the result that ministers were often compelled to read the burial service from a comfortable distance. Thomas Pennant describes a poors' hole in the churchyard of St. Giles's in the Fields: "In the church-yard I have observed with horror a great square pit, with many rows of coffins piled one upon the other, all exposed to sight and smell. Some of the piles were incomplete, expecting the mortality of the night. I turned away disgusted at the view, and scandalized at the want of police, which so little regards the health of the living as to permit so many putrid corpses, tacked between some slight boards, dispensing their dangerous effluvia over the capital" (*Some Ac-*

count of London, p. 175). There are also instances of churches being afflicted by the smell of corpses rising up from the crypt beneath the congregation. Memories of the plague charnel houses had still not disappeared. With public executions and public exhibitions of heads and quarters as well as bodies hung in irons, it is clear that the eighteenth-century confronted its mortality in a way that was both intense and direct.

In addition to air pollution and offensive smells, the eighteenth-century Londoner was subjected to what would seem to be an intolerable amount (and volume) of street noise. The clattering of horses' hooves and the rumbling of iron carriage, cart, and wagon wheels shaking the ground would be constants to which many other sounds would be added: ballad singers who congregated in circles at street corners (some even singing obscene songs in such environs as St. Paul's Churchyard, sometimes until as late as 11 P.M.) and hawkers of ballads; scavengers with carts and bells; bell-ringing collectors for the penny post; vendors of apples, pies, fish, or quack medicines; the cries of beggars, of chimney sweeps, and of link boys. The Thames watermen were particularly vociferous when seeking customers. There were town criers and milkwomen, whose cries were almost like a yodel.

Knife sharpeners subjected Londoners both to their cries and to the sounds of their grinding wheels. Less common (though obviously very important to Hogarth) were the sounds of puppeteers and of strolling players and musicians. It is easy to forget the normal sounds generated by families, children, church belfries, and domestic animals, but they would be there also, and in congested areas they would be there in abundance. Saussure complains that "Englishmen are mighty swearers . . . I consider this as another of their defects" (*A Foreign View of England,* p. 193). He complains in particular of British naval officers: "The greater number were the most debauched, the most dissolute, and the most terrible swearers I had ever come across" (p. 360). The pious and the delicate would no doubt be offended by the language of London streets with some regularity.

Those unlucky enough to be near burning buildings would

Hogarth: The sounds of London streets. Note the adult dress of the children and the swaddled child.

hear the sound of molten lead dripping to the street. Lead dripping from or running down buildings was a characteristic noted by observers of the great fire. Falling buildings, resulting often from cheap and hasty construction, were not unusual, and, as was already indicated, heavy, pendulous shop signs could sometimes accelerate the process. The creaking of the shop signs in the winds was but another sound with which the eighteenth-century Londoner would be all too familiar.

Johnson once described the manner in which the impact of the city's size could best be experienced: "Sir, if you wish to have a just notion of the magnitude of this city, you must not be satisfied with seeing its great streets and squares, but must survey the innumerable little lanes and courts. It is not in the showy evolutions of buildings, but in the multiplicity of human habitations which are crouded together, that the wonderful immensity of London consists" (*Life,* 1:421–22). Immensity sometimes holds a special appeal for those from small towns and villages. The immensity of London was undeniable, but that immensity was not an unmixed blessing. Fielding provides a different perspective on the lanes and courts to which Johnson was attracted: "Whoever indeed considers the Cities of *London* and *Westminster,* with the late vast Addition of their Suburbs; the great Irregularity of their Buildings, the immense Number of Lanes, Alleys, Courts and Bye-places; must think, that, had they been intended for the very Purpose of Concealment, they could scarce have been better contrived. Upon such a View, the whole appears as a vast Wood or Forest, in which a Thief may harbour with as great Security, as wild Beasts do in the Desarts of *Africa* or *Arabia*" (*An Enquiry into the Causes of the late Increase of Robbers,* p. 76). The city had become honeycombed with what were intended to be temporary dwellings but which grew to be permanent ones. The scarce available land was continually subdivided. Courts were built upon. Business establishments were cut up into tenements. Hovels and shacks were commonplace. Many of the poor crowded into deserted houses. A sizeable number of the city's inhabitants both lived and worked below ground level.

Johnson's comments on the city are largely favorable, but he was not blind to the city's condition. In a parliamentary debate on an abortive paving bill he puts the following remarks in the mouth of Lord Tyrconnel:

> The filth, sir, of some parts of the town, and the inequality and ruggedness of others, cannot but in the eyes of foreigners disgrace our nation, and incline them to imagine us a people, not only without delicacy, but without government, a herd of barbarians, or a colony of hottentots.
>
> The most disgusting part of the character given by travellers, of the most savage nations, is their neglect of cleanliness, of which, perhaps, no part of the world affords more

Temple Bar.

proofs, than the streets of the British capital; a city famous for wealth, and commerce, and plenty, and for every other kind of civility and politeness, but which abounds with such heaps of filth, as a savage would look on with amazement.

If that be allowed which is generally believed, that putrefaction and stench are the causes of pestilential distempers, the removal of this grievance may be pressed from motives of far greater weight than those of delicacy and pleasure . . .

That the present neglect of cleansing and paving the streets is such as ought not to be borne, that the passenger is every where either surprised and endangered by unexpected chasms, or offended and obstructed by mountains of filth, is well known to every one that has passed a single day in this great city; and that this grievance is without remedy is a sufficient proof that no magistrate has, at present power to remove it. [1825 *Works*, 10:239–41]

This, however, was not the only London which Johnson saw. When he arrived in London, the Thames' only bridge was London Bridge. As in medieval times, houses still stood on this bridge, a bridge rich in memory and tradition. Within the tower at its Southwark end there had been a cauldron in which the heads and quarters of traitors were cooked to preserve them from decay. The heads were then piked on the defenses of the bridge. Johnson would see the construction of Westminster Bridge and write proposals for the best method of erecting Blackfriars Bridge.

Johnson was to know a London which would grow with great rapidity and which would undergo palpable improvements. The Fleet River had been bridged over to make way for Fleet Market. In the 1760s the remaining portion of the Fleet would be covered to make an approach to Blackfriars Bridge. The Fleet had always been a source of filth and stench. The Carmelite friars had complained of the smell in the thirteenth century, and the nearby butchers, tanners, and cooks had polluted it over the years. Privies had been positioned above it as late as the mid-seventeenth century; in effect it functioned as an open sewer. In 1703 a man was found frozen, standing in the mud of Fleet Ditch. Johnson would see all this be changed.

In the 1760s the City gates were taken down to improve the flow of traffic, but Temple Bar, a site for great traffic jams, would not be removed until 1879. Shop signs were removed or placed flat; raised footpaths replaced the line of protective posts, and roadways were improved. By the later eighteenth century travelers to Paris would be shocked by the city's filth, just as French travelers to England had been appalled at the sight of similar filth in London in the earlier part of the century.

To speak of "Johnson's" London is to speak of a city in constant transition, but it is easy to exaggerate those changes which the inhabitants of the city experienced. The press of tradition, memory, and association was strong. Boswell came to the city in the 1760s filled with associations of London and Mr. Spectator, of London and Gay's Macheath. Living in Greenwich and working at St. John's Gate, Johnson found himself amidst associations with the peasants' rebellions. Wat Tyler's rebels (in 1381) and Jack Cade's (in 1450) had rallied on Blackheath Common in Greenwich, and the Priory buildings of the Knights of St. John were burned by Tyler's followers. The constitutionally rebellious Johnson found himself in fit locales.

Johnson might live in the London of clubs and coffee houses, of Cavendish, Hanover, Berkeley, and Grosvenor Squares, of Ranelagh and Vauxhall, but his spirit was often with the Renaissance, with its writers and its scholars. And while he knew and enjoyed the old, he looked forward to the new; he looked forward to meeting the young who were inheriting a London far different from that which he had himself inherited. The processes of change may be charted and detailed; in Johnson's imagination "London" existed as part of a continuum. To order and separate its events is necessary, but we should not forget the manner in which all could be present to an eye such as Johnson's.

In structuring his life, Johnson paid particular attention to the liturgical cycle. Curiously, he worshiped at St. Clement Danes in the Strand. Gough Square, Bolt Court, and Johnson's Court were in the parish of St. Dunstan's, but Johnson neither attended there nor at St. Bride's. There is mention of his going to St. Paul's and to the Temple Church, but his preference was for St. Clement's. His pew, number 18 in the north gallery, is near the pulpit.

Most of Johnson's London life was spent in the City, in the area of Fleet Street. Here is Boswell's list of his residences, enriched by notes of Hill, Powell, and others:

1. Exeter Street, off Catherine Street, Strand. March 1737.
2. Greenwich. July 1737. In Church Street, next door to the Golden Heart (Dobson, *Side-walk Studies*, p. 151).
3. Woodstock Street, near Hanover Square. End of 1737.
4. Castle Street, Cavendish Square, no. 6. Spring and October 1738 and January 1740. Now Castle Street East, Oxford Street.
5. Strand.

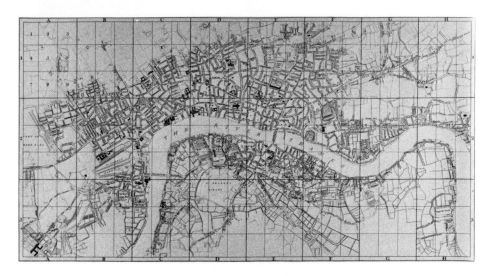

Rocque's map, with details. The details opposite are segments of the overview sketch above. Thus, A1 consists of the nine numbered blocks in the upper left-hand corner.

6. Boswell Court. (Carey Street, Lincoln's Inn Fields.) Boswell Court ran from Carey Street to the back of St. Clement Danes.
7. Strand. March 1741. "At the Black Boy, over against Durham Yard." The Adelphi was erected on Durham Yard.
8. Bow Street.
9. Holborn.
10. Fetter Lane.
11. Holborn, perhaps at the Golden Anchor near Holborn Bar.
12. Gough Square, no. 17. From at least July 1749 to March 1759. This residence, which alone survives, was the locus for Johnson's work on the *Dictionary*, the *Rambler*, the *Adventurer*, and *Rasselas*.
13. Staple Inn. March 1759.
14. Gray's Inn. November and December 1759.
15. Inner Temple Lane, no. 1. August 1760–July 1765. He occupied the first floor.
16. Johnson's Court, no. 7, Fleet Street. September 1765–

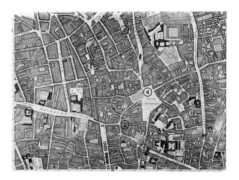

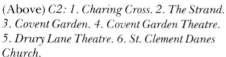

(Above) *C2: 1. Charing Cross. 2. The Strand. 3. Covent Garden. 4. Covent Garden Theatre. 5. Drury Lane Theatre. 6. St. Clement Danes Church.*

(Top right) *D2 (upper portion): 1. Temple Bar. 2. St. Dunstan's Church. 3. Gough Square. 4. Dung Wharf. 5. St. Bride's Church. 6. Bridewell. 7. Fleet Ditch. 8. Fleet Prison. 9. St. Paul's Cathedral.*

(Middle right) *D1 (lower portion): 1. Staple Inn. 2. Cock Lane. 3. Newgate Prison. 4. Smithfield Market. 5. St. John's Gate.*

(Bottom right) *E1 (lower portion): 1. Grub Street. 2. Bedlam Hospital. 3. The Guildhall.*

March 1776. Not named for Samuel, but rather for Thomas Johnson, an Elizabethan merchant taylor.

17. Bolt Court, no. 8, Fleet Street. March 1776–December 1784.

Johnson would also be staying with the Thrales at Streatham, at Southwark, at Grosvenor Square, or in Argyle Street. Many contemporary associations are connected with the Gough Square residence, since that is the one to survive, through the generosity of Lord Harmsworth, as a museum. The Inner Temple Lane residence (pulled down in 1857) is, however, the setting for many Boswell associations. Johnson lived there at the time of their first meeting, for example, and this was the place to which Bennet Langton and Topham Beauclerk came for their "frisk" with Johnson.

We cannot enter Johnson's mind, but we can reconstruct some of the associations which he would have felt in the area of Fleet Street and the Strand. The Temple, of course, is associated with the law and lawyers, but so was Gray's Inn and Staple Inn, originally an assembly point for wool merchants but later a residence for legal students. In immediate proximity to the lawyers of the Temple were the law breakers of Alsatia, a place of sanctuary, like the Mint in Southwark, named after the war-ravaged borderland of France and Germany. Alsatia was at its most lawless state in the seventeenth and very early eighteenth centuries.

The Fleet Street area had been ravaged by the great fire, and the plague had been particularly merciless, especially in the area near St. Bride's. Fleet Street was a very popular place for riots and demonstrations. In the Wilkes riots of 1763 a huge jackboot, ridiculing Bute, was burned at Temple Bar. During a Jacobite mughouse riot Mrs. Read's coffeehouse in Salisbury Court had been destroyed. The Fleet prison, a debtors' prison, was burned by the Gordon rioters. Within the prison's liberties (specified limits), taverners often had parsons on the premises to perform quick weddings. They were on retainer for 20 shillings a week (or more) and had touts to bring in the couples. "Fleet weddings" were used to bilk heirs and heiresses. The

Johnson's Home in Bolt Court.

St. Bride's, with St. Paul's in the background.

"officials" there falsified records, back-dated weddings, or obliterated records of them. This practice was not confined to the area of the Fleet; irregular marriages were performed in many locations before legislation inhibited the practice.

We do not associate the Fleet Street area with the theatre, but Johnson certainly would have. There were theatres in Whitefriars. The Salisbury Court Theatre perished in the fire, while that at Dorset Garden flourished in the Restoration. Salisbury Square was a kind of drama colony. Otway (who, with Lee was buried in St. Clement's) lived nearby, as did Lady Davenant, who is buried in St. Bride's. Shadwell lived there with his wife (an actress), and so did such actors as Harris, Underhill, and Betterton. Many other literary personages were associated with the district. Milton lived in St. Bride's churchyard, Richardson in Salisbury Square, Dryden in Salisbury Court and Fetter Lane. Walton lived in Fleet Street by the corner of Chancery Lane and was a vestryman of St. Dunstan's Church. Goldsmith lived in the Temple and in Wine Office Court near

Gough Square. Lovelace had lived in Gunpowder Alley, Drayton in Fleet Street, Hobbes in Fetter Lane. Locke dated his *Essay* from Dorset (Salisbury) Court. Ben Jonson's club had met at the Devil Tavern in the Apollo Chamber (actually the Devil and St. Dunstan's Tavern, St. Dunstan being the patron of the goldsmiths' art). Swift dined at the Devil with Addison, and the poets laureate sometimes rehearsed their court-day odes in the Apollo Chamber.

Printers and booksellers had long been associated with the area. Wynkyn de Worde's printing house was in St. Bride's parish. Richard Tottel (known then as a legal printer, known now more for his *Miscellany*) was in Fleet Street, near the Middle Temple Gate. John Hodgets, at Fleet Street and Fetter Lane, issued the plays of such writers as Dekker, Webster, and Haywood. Jacob Tonson was in Chancery Lane, a few doors from Fleet Street. Lintot was in Fleet Street, west of Inner Temple Gate, Motte near Temple Bar. Curll kept on the move, but at various times he was in and around the Fleet Street area. One of the very first English lending libraries was established in 1740 by a bookseller in the Strand. (Circulating libraries consisted largely of nonfiction, but the greatest demand was for fiction—particularly ephemeral fiction—with theatrical publications coming in second.)

First and foremost Fleet Street was religious in its associations. The Blackfriars had arrived at their Thames location in 1276. The Carmelite settlement at Whitefriars was there before it was destroyed by Henry VIII. The Knights Templars had first lodged in Holborn (as had the Blackfriars) but moved to New Temple in 1184. Their order (originally founded to protect pilgrims from robbers in the Holy Land) was there until its suppression in 1310. In the reign of Edward III the Temple was leased to students of the common law. The Templars claimed allegiance to the pope alone and declared their independence of any other episcopal rule. The Temple Church numbered among its relics wood from the true cross, some of Christ's blood, and the sword which killed Thomas à Becket. Pilgrimages were conducted to the church.

As one goes farther back in history, as the eighteenth-century writer did in his imagination, the associations are, of course, Roman. A Roman bath, probably attached to the home of a Roman noble, was found just beyond St. Clement Danes Church. Thus, what for us is a district of small shops dominated by the newspaper industry was, for Johnson, an area of law and lawlessness, of religious faith and public disturbances, of fire and plague, of books and theatres, of prisons and churches, and, especially, an area wherein one walked with the ghosts of the great writers of England. What it sacrificed to Westminster in style and fashion it matched with inestimable cultural richness. There is little surprise that Johnson was attached to it.

II. Work and Money

To think of London is to think of trade, for the city was established as a center for trade; military and governmental considerations were secondary. Situated on a tidal river which was quickly bridged and resting on an island near the coast of continental Europe, London became a pivotal part of the European economic community. By the eighteenth century London's intellectual and cultural competitor was still Paris, but it had eclipsed its only major economic competitor, Amsterdam, in the seventeenth century. Centuries before, the Phoenicians had come to trade in tin. The Romans had come and the Saxons and Danes. The Lombards had come and the Flemish merchants, who had heard of the excellence of English wool. Many of the Dutch had accompanied William, and many of the Germans, the Hanoverians.

By A.D. 359 there were 800 vessels in London engaged in the coal trade. By the twelfth century the citizen of London could purchase Arabian gold, weapons from Scythia, precious gems from Egypt, silk from China, French wine, and Russian sable. Companies of foreign merchants established headquarters in London (St. Clement Danes, where Johnson worshipped, recalls the Danish colony which existed in the city). By the fourteenth century London was the center of the wool trade, by the fifteenth the center of the cloth trade. By the late sixteenth century her position was secured, for the discovery of the New World had placed London at the center of world trade rather than at a point on its fringes.

By the eighteenth century London was important in various respects and known for various activities. It was the center of inland trade, a center through which many materials came. Textiles, for example, were sent to London to be dyed and

London after the great fire.

pressed. The city was known for its breweries and distilleries, its clothing and silk industries. Ships were built there, as were coaches. London was well-known for its leather goods. Watches were made there, as was jewelry, furniture, and plate.

The economic strength of the city had been tested severely by the great fire. Beginning in a baker's house in Pudding Lane, the fire burned from 2 September till 6 September 1666. A strong east wind carried sparks to a pile of hay in an inn yard opposite the lane. The flames spread to Thames Street, where stores of flammable oil and spirits were kept in cellars. On the open wharves nearby were stacks of timber, coal, and hay. The fire spread easily. Moreover, the summer had been hot and dry; the wooden buildings were consumed quickly. Only about one-sixth of the walled city survived, and the area beyond the wall which was lost was approximately equal to the area inside which was saved. Most of the public and commercial buildings were lost, as were 13,200 houses and shops, St. Paul's, and nearly 90 churches. Warehouses, filled with goods, were de-

The forest of ships' masts at London docks. The Tower is in the background.

stroyed, goods—we must remember—that were uninsured.
Evelyn describes the sight:

> The fountaines dried up & ruind, whilst the very waters
> remained boiling; the Voragos of subterranean Cellars
> Wells & Dungeons, formerly Warehouses, still burning in
> stench & dark clowds of smoke like hell, so as in five or six
> miles traversing about, I did not see one loade of timber
> unconsum'd, nor many stones but what were calcind white as
> snow, so as the people who now walked about the ruines,
> appeard like men in some dismal desart, or rather in some
> greate Citty, lay'd wast by an impetuous & cruel Enemy, to
> which was added the stench that came from some poore
> Creatures bodys, beds, & other combustible goods. [*Diary,* pp.
> 498–99]

Despite the devastation, merchants met their foreign obliga-
tions, and London was rebuilt within little more than four

years, a sign of the will and courage of the city, underwritten by incredible economic resilience.

In Johnson's London, the commercial vigor of the city was evident in the traffic on the Thames. Coal came from Newcastle; lumber came from Scotland or the Baltic. Beneath London Bridge there was a forest of ships' masts. The terminus for much of this trade was the London shop, a hallmark of London life both in Johnson's time and in our own. Grosley, touring in 1765, thought that the Strand, Fleet Street, and Cheapside shops were "the most striking objects that London [could] offer to the eye of a stranger" (*A Tour to London,* 1:35). Travelers were particularly struck by the windows of the shops. Moritz (1782) described a street of London shops as "a well-arranged show-cabinet" (*Journeys of a German in England,* pp. 190–91).

In the early decades of the century Saussure had wandered by the Strand, Fleet Street, and Cheapside shops and was just as impressed as Moritz: "Every house, or rather every shop, has a sign of copper, pewter, or wood painted and gilt. Some of these signs are really magnificent, and have cost as much as one hundred pounds sterling; they hang on big iron branches, and sometimes on gilt ones. . . . A stranger might spend whole days, without ever feeling bored, examining these wonderful goods [in the shop windows]" (*A Foreign View of England,* p. 81).

What was striking was not just the quantity and quality of goods but their exposure to public view: the fact that large sums were invested in advertising and that the risk of burglary did not seem to trouble the tradesmen. We must remember the economic extremes which were an everyday fact of eighteenth-century life. Boswell walked into Thomas Jefferys' shop on Cockspur Street, Charing Cross, and purchased a sword for five guineas. Five guineas might well be more than an industrious laborer would earn in three months. The fact that expensive goods sat in open view of often very poor passersby was surprising to many. London was in some ways like a museum whose treasures were exhibited with very little attention to security.

At mid-century the leading tradesmen were located in Pall

Cheapside shops and St. Mary le Bow Church. Note shop signs.

Mall, St. Paul's Churchyard, and the Strand; there the wealthy shopped. With the exception of Somerset and Northumberland Houses, the Strand consisted entirely of shops and constituted London's principal street for shopping. The shops were small. There were no department stores and very few branch shops. Most tradesmen lived behind their shops with their families and apprentices; only the rich would have separate private dwellings. Tradesmen advertised in newspapers and also issued cards. These were often packed with goods or used to record prices for potential customers doing comparison shopping. Many of the trade cards survive and are an excellent introduction to an important part of the economic life of eighteenth-century London.

The types of shops which one might encounter would be many. Moritz writes that the most frequent inscription on Strand shop signs was "Dealer in Foreign Spirituous Liquors" (*Journeys of a German in England,* p. 33), but he would have passed many other kinds of shops. There were, to give only a few examples, pewterers, grocers, and wire workers; ironmongers (who would sell kettles, pots, and probably pens,

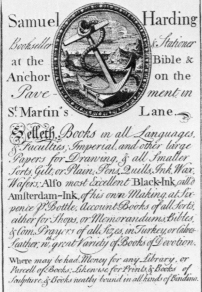
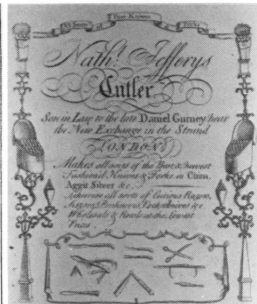

Tradesmen's cards.

watches, and jewelry), furriers, painters, tobacconists, milliners, and haberdashers. There were shops specializing in lamps and lanterns, in paper hangings, and in prints. There were cutlers (like Jefferys), cabinetmakers and upholsterers, glovers, druggists, linen drapers, and goldsmiths, the latter, pillars of the city's economic community. One would see stationers, seedsmen, cartographers, and mathematical instrument makers. Some shops were localized. Harness makers, for example, tended to locate near the Royal Mews in Charing Cross, and were seldom seen in the Strand.

"Specialties" can be confusing. Many shops, for example, operated undertaking businesses. A stationer might sell ladies' whalebone stays or silver sand boxes for drying ink. Toymen would sell jewelry, trinkets, buckles, bric-a-brac, and snuff boxes as well as toys. Of particular importance was the chandler, who sold (besides candles) fast foods: bread, cheese, and small beer, generally at prices lower than those which one would encounter at an alehouse. The chandler also sold such things as coal, links, soap, and sand. He dealt in small quantities and was thus of greater importance to the poor than to the opulent.

In addition to the stylish and attractive shops there were far humbler enterprises: bulkhead shops, for example, or the selling of items from baskets or wheelbarrows. There were itinerant salesmen and saleswomen then as now, none perhaps more famous than Tiddy Doll, the gingerbread seller, who stands in the foreground in plate 11 of Hogarth's *Industry and Idleness*, hawking his wares at Tyburn. Booksellers set out stalls to display their books, but were sometimes set upon by poor yet curious readers who read the books at the stalls without paying for them. If they were confronted, such readers would move to another establishment and another stall and pick up where they had left off. Some would even turn down a page or mark a place so that they could return at a more auspicious time to complete their chapter or volume.

The hours were long. Most shops opened at eight (some earlier) and stayed open until eight at night (some even later). The rewards of a successful business would be many, but the work was not easy. Defoe writes that "customers love to see the master's face in the shop, and to go to a shop where they are sure to find him at home" (*The Complete English Tradesman*, letter 5). There should be very little delegation of responsibility. Defoe's image describing the life of trade is not easily forgotten:

> Trade is like a hand-mill, it must always be turned about by the diligent hand of the master: or, if you will, like the pump-house at Amsterdam, where they put offenders in for petty matters, especially beggars; if they will work and keep pumping, they sit well and dry and safe; and if they work very hard one hour or two, they may rest, perhaps, a quarter of an hour afterwards, but if they oversleep themselves, or grow lazy, the water comes in upon them and wets them, and they have no dry place to stand in, much less to sit down in; and in short, if they continue obstinately idle, they must sink,

Bulkhead shops.

so that it is nothing but *pump* or *drown,* and they may chuse
which they like best. [Ibid.]

Defoe's judgment may be severe, but it was not uninformed.
Born the son of a tallow-chandler, Defoe was an experienced

merchant, working as a hosier who also dealt in wine, tobacco, and other commodities.

Despite the vitality of London's economy, work was not always easily found. The problem was particularly acute for women. Many turned to prostitution because of limited opportunity elsewhere. The income was, of course, a powerful inducement. A fourteen- to sixteen-hour day as a seamstress, which would yield pennies, was not an attractive alternative. A woman could hawk fruit or fish, sell milk, or carry loads from markets. There were some female butchers and weavers, but in general a woman would be paid markedly less than a man for similar work. Generally a woman could not teach unless she had the funds to first set up a school. Positions as servants were not always available. Many girls came to London from the country seeking such employment. Their coaches were often met by procurers who led them into lives of prostitution.

Many unskilled occupations were taken by Irish immigrants, who also made up a sizeable portion of the large number of London beggars. In the late 1760s and early 1770s there were perhaps as many as 15,000 black slaves in the country as well, so that employment for unskilled laborers was not as readily available as one might assume. Thus, many chose to emigrate to America as indentured servants. Generally they served four years in return for their passage and found themselves in a position not unlike that of the transported felon, who served seven to fourteen years.

An alternative chosen by many (or one to which many were forced) was begging in London streets. Saussure saw them continually "in all the streets and highways of London" (*A Foreign View of England*, pp. 187–88). He encountered a man who made a living by simulating being crippled and hence enhanced his ability to secure alms from passersby (pp. 188–89). Archenholz recounts an experience which was not uncommon:

> A friend of mine who wished to see and converse with all descriptions of men, having one day put on a ragged coat, promised to reward a mendicant if he would conduct him

thither. He was accordingly introduced, found a great deal of gaiety and ease, and nothing that bore the appearance of indigence, save the tatters that covered the members. One cast his crutches into a corner of the room; one unbuckled his wooden leg; another took of [*sic*] the plaister which concealed his eye; all, in fine discovered themselves in their own natural forms; recounted the adventures of that day, and concerted the stratagems to be put in execution on the morrow. . . .

The female beggars generally hire infants from those who are poorer than themselves, to rouse, by that means, the charity of the passengers. They pay various prices for these children, from sixpence to two shillings a day, according as they are more or less deformed. A child that is very crooked and distorted generally earns three shillings, and sometimes even more. [*A Picture of England,* p. 73]

Many poor children were intentionally blinded or maimed in order to increase their success as beggars. Poor children who were abandoned by their parents often fell into the lives of pickpockets or prostitutes (some at the age of nine or ten); some had their teeth removed to be sold to the rich. Abandonment appears to have been more common than infanticide, but many children were killed with brandy, Hungary water, gin, rum, or opium-based nostrums. In some poor families infants were given drugs to keep them quiet while their mothers left the home to work.

We must remember that for the poor, child labor was a donnée. The laborer was often unable to support a family on his wages; the wife and children were forced to work. One characteristically English occupation, and one particularly associated with the eighteenth-century child, was that of the chimney sweep. The life of the sweep was a very difficult (though often mercifully short) one. Many were as young as four years old when they began to work as sweeps. Most never bathed and, of course, contracted serious skin disease as a result. Because of their constant contact with carcinogenic soot, they often suffered from cancer of the scrotum—an

Hogarth: A Tyburn execution. Tiddy Doll stands in the foreground selling gingerbread.

occupational hazard associated with the life of the sweep. The most profitable work of a sweep was the extinguishing of chimney fires, the profit arising from its danger. Many sweeps were suffocated in the process of quelling such fires. There are accounts of sweeps having their feet pricked with pins when they hesitated to go up the chimneys. In some cases fires were set beneath them if they balked in their task.

The English economy was built upon a good bit of brutality and cruelty. For example, one of the "prizes" of the Treaty of Utrecht was that England received a major share of the slave trade. The Africa Company undertook to deliver a minimum of 4,800 slaves per year, with one-fourth of the profits going to the king of Spain and one-fourth to Queen Anne. Between 1680 and 1780 the British imported over two million slaves to her colonies in America and the West Indies. In 1771, for example, 58 slave ships sailed from London, 107 from Liverpool, and 23 from Bristol. They transported 50,000 slaves. While the slaves were freed in England in 1772, some Englishmen were especially troubled by the treatment of slaves in the colonies. Wesley noted that advertisements in North Carolina and Virginia newspapers for runaway slaves offered more money for the slave's severed head than for his return alive. Johnson's forthright and unceasing condemnation of the slave trade (both in England and in the colonies) is often pointed to by Johnson scholars.

In addition to beggars, sweeps, slaves, and prostitutes, another familiar London sight was the apprentice—much maligned for his idleness, indolence, and thievery. He was there in numbers. Perhaps 20,000 to 30,000 bachelor apprentices would be found at a given time, and they constituted a ready clientele for the London prostitutes. Boys were bound until the age of twenty-four (twenty-one in 1767 for London), girls until marriage or the age of twenty-one (twenty-four outside of London until 1778). The notion of training in the hands of an established professional appears to be a good one and there are notable success stories, but the opportunity for abuse was considerable. In many cases children were simply drudges; some were little more than slaves. Some were killed, even tortured to death by such cruel masters and mistresses as Elizabeth Brownrigg, who was hanged in 1767 for her crimes. Masters were tempted to take on children (and thus receive fees) to aid themselves in their present circumstances with no regard for the future of the child. As Dorothy George argues (*London Life in the Eighteenth Century*, p. 228), the system was seriously flawed in its very conception, for the child was likely to be either a nuisance and a drag on the operation or a skilled individual with little patience for years of drudgery. It would be difficult to sustain fruitful and amicable working relationships under either circumstance. The large number of runaway apprentices should therefore occasion little surprise. The London businessman could not entrust his work to others, as Defoe pointed out, the result being a continual state of intense preoccupation. Grosley describes such Londoners: "The English walk very fast: their thoughts being entirely engrossed by business, they are very punctual to their appointments, and those, who happen to be in their way, are sure to be sufferers by it: constantly darting forward, they justle them with a force proportioned to their bulk and the velocity of their motion" (*A Tour to London*, 1:105).

Perhaps the most surprising aspect of eighteenth-century life, particularly in light of the fact that the period produced so much art and intelligence, is the fact that the government took no responsibility for education. Even as late as 1837 only one in ten went to school. Oxford and Cambridge were little more than pleasant clubs in the eighteenth century, and very few students even got there. Some poor children attended Sunday schools and charity schools, both of which were determined to teach the poor the virtue of staying in their place. There were probably no more than 40,000 children attending charity schools at any one time. Those who could afford it attended public schools, grammar schools or dame schools. The last were very uneven in quality. "Public school" and "grammar school" denoted a school with an endowment and a governing board, as opposed to a private school, which was run by a single individual. Students at the dame schools were often taught by individuals with other jobs. Standards and qualifications were not given serious attention. The dissenters (non-Anglican English Protestants) established their own academies, many of which were extremely effective. Indeed, some Anglicans sent their sons there.

The charity schools taught the beliefs of the Church of England and provided some instruction in reading, writing, and arithmetic (girls were often taught sewing instead of mathematics). At the grammar schools the paramount concern was with Latin, although there was sometimes instruction in Hebrew and Greek. Writing and arithmetic were not stressed. At a public school such as Eton in the 1760s students would learn grammar, composition, Latin, Greek, and some history and geography. They might read Pope, Milton, the *Spectator*, and Greek and Roman history, give speeches and draw maps. Hours were long. On holidays and half-holidays they might take short lessons in mathematics, algebra, geography, drawing, and French, possibly also some dancing and fencing. At Oxford and Cambridge education was little more than the continuation of classical studies begun in school. The rudiments of logic, metaphysics, astronomy, and natural philosophy were also taught.

For women "accomplishments" were more important than education. Whether educated in school or by governesses, young girls were taught such things as sewing, knitting, and spinning. Lace-making was viewed as being of nearly equal importance with reading and writing. Women might also learn cooking, some French and Italian, and music, particularly performance on the piano. That the period produced excellent women writers and scholars—many of them Johnson's friends and colleagues—is a tribute to individual courage and enterprise, not to the "system" of eighteenth-century education. Had there been far more education it is quite possible that there would have been far fewer prisons, gaols, and Bridewells. Johnson's support for education was unflagging.

Early eighteenth-century coinage consisted of the following pieces: in gold, the five guinea, two guinea, guinea, and half guinea; in silver, the crown, half crown, shilling, sixpence, fourpence, threepence, twopence, and penny; in copper, the half pence and farthing. Values were as follows:

4 farthings = 1 penny (abbreviated d.)
12 pence = 1 shilling (abbreviated s. or /; thus, 3/6 equals 3 shillings, sixpence)
2s. 6d. = a half crown
20s. = 1 pound (£)
21s. = 1 guinea

Conversion to modern values is difficult for a number of reasons. One is modern inflation in the United Kingdom: estimates given in books written in the 1960s are meaningless for the 1980s. Also, the "equivalents" can be misleading in that certain items are far cheaper today than they were in the eighteenth century (because of, for example, mass production), and some are far more expensive (artworks, for example). I find Mary Hyde's method (*The Thrales of Streatham Park*, p. 12) a good one: "Eighteenth-century figures should be multiplied by twenty to give an idea of present value—that is to say in the 1960s, before escalating inflation." Figures should be doubled (at least) to correct for inflation. Thus the £600 which Johnson thought would provide a life of splendor would equal £24,000 or $50,000, today, and it would not provide a life of splendor in central London.

We should not forget the matter of economic extremes between classes. In a letter to Baretti in 1762 Johnson writes that "Mr. Reynolds gets six thousand a year" (*Letters*, vol. 1, no. 142), £240,000, or $500,000, in modern currency. A laborer at the time might make £25 a year, which would be £1,000, or $2,200, today. The gap between wages is narrower today, just as the distance from extreme poverty to great wealth is shorter. Thus it is not always useful to "convert" to modern currency. For example, we sometimes hear of the rule of thumb that a book always costs approximately what a meal costs, but a poor Londoner might eat at an ordinary for 2½d. while a member of Johnson's Club might find the bill for a meal to average out at £1 4s. per person (with a contemporary novel costing 2s. 6d. to 3s. for a 300-page twelve-mo).

Another factor must be calculated into the bargain also: London prices. Archenholz writes that there are two things necessary for the man who would stay in England: a knowledge of the language and "plenty of money, to enable him to live comfortably in a country where every thing is dear" (*A Picture of England*, p. 3). Grosley comments that "every thing there is exceeding dear; but it is equally so to the English themselves and to foreigners" (*A Tour to London*, 1:10). Rochefoucauld, who toured in 1784, puts it succinctly: "Everything costs twice as much here as in France" (*A Frenchman in England*, p. 30). Travelers from North America learn this lesson today. Goods (with some notable exceptions) often cost twice in London what they would elsewhere, so that giving dollar equivalencies for sterling is misleading. The traveler's $10, which would be exchanged for £4–£5, will buy goods costing $4–$5 in North America; and the burden is not carried equally by the Londoner (as Grosley wrote), for the Londoner's salary is likely to be far less than that of his North American counterpart and his taxes higher (another factor which skews salary comparisons between the eighteenth century and the twentieth).

Salaries and fees were subject to fluctuation of various kinds. For example, many prices rose in the course of the century, and many salaries failed to keep pace with inflation. A year with massive crop failure due to adverse weather could bring death by starvation and malnutrition to many of the London poor. Much employment was seasonal. Workmen were not only affected by the weather but also by the fact that the wealthy left London for three to four months of every year. The economic dislocation which results from alternation between a wartime and peacetime economy was another significant factor. Between 1695 and 1815 England was at peace for fifty-seven years, at war for sixty-three years. Thus it would be quite common for a workman to receive good wages at very irregular intervals. With this would come idleness and, very often, drunkenness. Many managers and foremen were in league with tavern keepers. Wages were paid in taverns and, in some cases, drunk up almost immediately. Some tavern keepers allowed poor workmen to drink well beyond their means. They took the man's note for the liquor and then sold it to an employer seeking someone with the poor man's skills. The man was then forced to work for the purchaser of the note without pay, his alternative being jail. The practice was termed "buying carcasses."

The tavern served a central function in the Londoner's life. At some times it took on special economic functions. In Pepys' London, for example, there was a chronic shortage of small change. To solve the problem tavern keepers (and many shopkeepers) issued their own tokens, which would be honored in the neighborhood by anyone who knew the issuer. These tokens also served as additional advertising for the establishment and (like the shop sign) were a counter to illiteracy, for the shop's or tavern's sign was stamped on one side, the street and initials of the issuer on the other. Tokens were issued in the eighteenth century also. In the later eighteenth century, probably around 1787–90, a halfpenny was struck by Henry Biggs of Moor Street, Birmingham, with a portrait of Johnson stamped upon it. The token was valid in Birmingham, Lichfield, and Wolverhampton (it is illustrated on page 46 of the Golden Jubilee Issue of the *New Rambler: Journal of the Johnson Society of London*). Such tokens were used for paying wages and were generally accepted in the neighborhood of the factory issuing them.

The absence of hard currency was a hardship felt by seamen, who might be paid in scrip redeemable in London. Naturally, they traded the scrip for a fraction of its value in ready money. Prior, working as a diplomatist for the government, was often paid in tallies, wooden sticks which were marked and notched to indicate value in sterling. These would be exchanged (at a loss) in return for ready money. We must remember also the number of highwaymen and footpads ready to relieve people of what money they did have. Mrs. Johnson sewed two guineas in her petticoat when her son Sam was taken to London to be touched by Queen Anne. Johnson says that she, "not having been accustomed to money, was afraid of such expenses as now seem very small" (*Diaries, Prayers, and Annals*, p. 9), but he is writing in retrospect, perhaps as much as sixty years later. The two guineas today would be worth slightly less than £100. Johnson and his mother returned in the stage wagon rather than the stage coach because of Johnson's cough. He thought his mother was trying to save a few shillings, but it is possible that fears of the highwayman were also on Mrs. Johnson's mind, for the poor traveled by wagon and the highwayman would expect more wealthy victims elsewhere. Women often traveled by wagon and these women would not be expected to have large sums with them.

Travel in general was an expensive activity in the eighteenth century. Johnson knew it in its possible extremes, having traveled in the stage wagon with his mother and toured France with the Thrales. According to Baretti's financial account, the trip of fifty-nine days cost Thrale 822 guineas (Hyde, *The Thrales of Streatham Park*, p. 141), or perhaps £35,000 in modern currency.

Prior to mass production both clothing and furniture were expensive. Wigs were very expensive: a mediocre peruke could easily cost a guinea. As such, they were a target for thieves. Some even cut holes in the hoods of closed carriages and stole the wigs from travelers' heads. A wig worth £30 (in eighteenth-century currency) was not uncommon. Yet many of the poor wore them along with their wealthy fellow citizens. Their clothing would come from secondhand stores (slop shops) and would be one of the few valuable items they were likely to possess. When a poor man was robbed it would generally be his clothing which was taken. Johnson, who showed how a man could live in London on £30 a year, paid as much for a new suit and wig for his trip to Paris.

Craftsmanship was prized, and very high prices could result from it. Kielmansegge, traveling in 1761–62, writes that "the Woodstock workmanship in steel is much preferred to that of Salisbury, and it is not unusual to find steel scissors, buckles, and watch-chains which cost from ten, fifteen, to thirty or more guineas" (*Diary of a Journey to England,* p. 93). Tea was expensive but a staple. Eden estimated that at the end of the century a laborer whose family income was only £40 a year would spend £2 just for tea. Its value was such that one of the servant's perquisites in a wealthy household was the ability to sell the family's used tea leaves to the poor.

The resident of eighteenth-century London would pay less for rent than his modern counterpart: perhaps 1s. 6d. per week for a cellar or garret, 2s. 6d. for a furnished room, both of these in poor sections. The gentleman would pay in guineas rather than shillings, particularly when he required quarters for a large number of servants. Moritz, in 1782, stayed with a tailor's widow near George Street. He had two rooms, both nicely furnished, on the ground floor. The rooms had carpets, leather chairs, and mahogany tables. For that he paid 16s. a week. In Oxford he paid 3s. for supper, bed, and breakfast, plus an additional shilling for the waiter. At Sutton he paid 1s. for supper, bed, and breakfast and 4d. to the daughter of the house for maid service, who then gave him a letter of recommendation for an inn at Lichfield, "for in general the people of Lichfield are haughty" (*Journeys of a German in England,* p. 148).

In 1762 Boswell drew up a "Scheme of Living." His allowance from his father was £200 a year. On rents he comments: "A genteel lodging in a good part of the town is absolutely necessary. These are very dear. None proper for me can be had under two guineas or a guinea and a half. But if I take it for a year, I think I may have it for £50" (*London Journal*, p. 335). He did find a place in Crown Street, Westminster, "an obscure street but pretty lodgings at only £22" (ibid., p. 58) and took it in an effort to save money: "I thought my seeking a lodging was like seeking a wife. Sometimes I aimed at one of two guineas a week, like a rich lady of quality. Sometimes at one guinea, like a knight's daughter; and at last fixed on £22 a year, like the daughter of a good gentleman of moderate fortune" (ibid., p. 59).

For his Gough Square residence Johnson probably paid about £18 a year rent plus taxes and tithes. The figure of £26 which is often cited would probably have included additional assessments (to St. Bride's, for street lighting, for the watch, for the poor-rate, and additional special claims, for example, to support orphans). In 1756 he was assessed 17s. 4d. for "cleaning repairing and beautifying the Church" (Clifford, *Dictionary Johnson*, pp. 21–22).

The cost of food is difficult to estimate because of market fluctuations. Burnett (*A History of the Cost of Living*, pp. 135–36) offers the following examples:

4-lb. loaf of bread	4d.–5d. early century; 6d.–7d. near the end
beer: small beer	1½ d./gal.
"middling"	2d./gal.
strong ale	4d./qt.
beef, veal, mutton, pork	2½d./lb.
fowls	1s. 4d./pair
rabbits	3d.
eggs	3 or 4 for a penny
potatoes	4d./peck at mid-century; more later
cabbage	½d. at mid-century; more later

| milk | 1d./qt. at mid-century; more later |
| Cheshire cheese | 2d.–2½d./lb. at mid-century; more later |

Ashton (*Social Life in the Reign of Queen Anne,* pp. 145–55) gives the following figures for the early century:

oysters	2s.–3s./barrel (very cheap and plentiful)
asses' milk	3s. 6d./qt.
ordinary claret	4s.–6s./gal. from the wood
good bottled claret	3s.–10s./bottle, probably more at a tavern
champagne	8s./bottle
black tea	12s.–28s./lb. in 1710
coffee	5s. 8d./lb in 1710
chocolate	2s.–3s./lb.

Grosley (*A Tour to London,* 1:67) encountered the following prices in 1765:

bread	2½d.–3d./lb.
coarse meat	4½d./lb.
roasting beef	8d.–9d./lb.
bacon	10d./lb.
butter	11d./lb.

It must be remembered that tavern food would include a sizable gratuity. Moritz, for example, dining at an eating house in 1782, paid 1s. for a little salad and some roast meat but gave nearly half a shilling to the waiter for service. One of the most important items in the working man's budget was beer. In the early part of the century Saussure found small beer at 1d. a pot, porter at 3d. a pot (porter—drunk by porters, presumably, who were strapping and thirsty—was stronger). Later in the century, after about 1761, porter would be 3½d. It has been estimated that consumption of beer (primarily by working classes) equalled approximately 35 gallons per person per year. Our eighteenth-century forbears did not drink water.

Approximately half of the population in the eighteenth century were agricultural laborers; many of these people made so little that they could not exist without charity. Thus, as Dorothy George writes, "Throughout the century it was accounted a great social service to find employment for women and children, since no labouring man could be expected to support a wife and family unaided" (*England in Transition,* p. 22). Before 1765 a London laborer might earn 9s.–12s. a week. Those with skills would do better. A printer, for example, might make £1 a week, while a jeweller or maker of optical instruments who could work quickly might draw £3–£4. Hours were long. A compositor, for example, might make 24s. a week, but he would work twelve-hour days, six days a week. Johnson probably paid his amanuenses on the Dictionary project 7s.–12s. a week, while Perkins, Thrale's right hand and the superintendent of his brewery, was paid £500 a year. Burnett (*A History of the Cost of Living,* pp. 181–84) gives the following salary estimates:

chair carver	perhaps £4/week
journeyman tailor	21s. 9d./week
Newcastle collier	15s./week
Sheffield cutlery worker	13s. 6d./week
porcelain workers	9s./week
weavers, spinners	8s. 7d./week (textile workers generally made less than others)
saddler	15s/week
masons, bricklayers, joiners	20d.–29d./day (1700–1790)
maids	£2–£4/year (which included lodging, generally in the garret —with the men in the cellar)
good butler	£20/year

On a wealthy estate a house staff, including gardeners and gamekeepers, might include as many as seventy individuals. Including board, lodging, and livery, the house steward might draw £100 a year, the clerk of the kitchen £60, the head keeper

£43, the head cook £40, and the housekeeper £28. Then the salaries plummeted, with a footman earning £8, a maid £4 (Burnett, pp. 143–44). A good wet nurse, on the other hand, might, at mid-century, make £25 a year.

Salaries, it need hardly be said, were not lavish. For the approximately four hundred families of the landed aristocracy the situation would be different. A wealthy man like the duke of Newcastle would be worth £40,000 a year, the equivalent of £1,600,000 a year in modern currency. The average income among the aristocracy might be closer to £10,000, with many "poor" peers receiving £3,000–£4,000. A bishopric such as Oxford or Bristol would be worth about £300 a year; the bishoprics of Winchester, Durham, or London, perhaps ten times that much. Members of the squierarchy might make anywhere from £200–£5,000 per year. Johnson's £300 pension would be about the same as the income of the average rural freeholder with a comparatively large farm.

The fees which one rank of people paid would, with the services received, be largely unknown to another rank. Still, it might be useful to indicate the kinds of fees, prices, and costs which different segments of the population would face. The following list is unsystematic but may be instructive:

A doctor might charge 10s. or more for a visit; a famous one (like Mead, whose fees came to about £7,000 per year) would charge more. Doctors were seldom called until the patient was dying. Four doses of Dr. James's famous fever powder would cost 2s. 6d.

Emigration to America from either London or Bristol cost £5. To educate your child at a grammar school would only cost a few guineas a year, because of the endowments. A private boarding school might cost as much as £30–£40 per year; a nonconformist academy like Warrington, £17 for commons, £3 3s. for an apartment, with extra fees for lectures.

A good saddle horse might cost 15 guineas; the stud fee for a good stallion, 5–10 guineas. A hunting horse could cost as much as 50 guineas. A good pair of hunting hounds could cost 10–12 guineas. The cottages of the poor, past which the horses and hounds would run, might cost £15–£20 to build. A two-bedroom cottage would cost £40–£50. Johnson's *Dictionary*, in two folio volumes and weighing approximately twenty-five pounds, cost £4 10s., while a cheap pocket edition of Milton in calf might be found for 2s. Christie, in the 1770s, might sell a Titian for 130 guineas. Johnson's library of 650 lots (not including the pictures) brought £247 and a few shillings.

To see Johnson's play *Irene* at Drury Lane cost the following: box seat, 5s.; pit, 3s.; first gallery, 2s.; upper gallery, 1s. In order to put on a play, the following expenses might be incurred: orchestra, £18–£20 per night (5s. more for kettledrums and French horns); candles, £3; 5s. for the theatre barber; 2s. 6d. for the box-office clerk; 15s. each for armed guards (an important expense); £3 6s. per day for the manager; £1 for theatre rent; and 3s. 6d. and up for advertising. Still the profits could be £100 a night. For the professional writer the theatre offered the best opportunity for financial success. Money could be made elsewhere, of course, but not so quickly or in such quantity.

Coal cost 25s.–32s. per chaldron (26–27 cwt.) at the beginning of the century, and 36s.–38s. at the end, but prices fluctuated depending on location: the bushel of coal that cost 5s. in London at the end of the century might cost 10d. in Bath. The modern reader should be cautioned about eighteenth-century measures. For example, a chaldron of coal in the 1670s was 36 heaped bushels, about 2,240 pounds. But 36 bushels in the eighteenth century would be closer to 2,000 pounds, while a Newcastle coal chalder was 72 heaped bushels, or 2 standard English chalders. Similarly, the stone as a unit of measure generally equalled 14 pounds, but it could vary between, say, 5 and 32 pounds, depending on the commodity being weighed.

Just as today, "prices" are approximations. The quality of the shop or store, its location and clientele, or the quality of a dining establishment will lead to great variance in price. The best way to approach individual economies is to study the manner in which budgets were drawn. For example, Boswell's "Scheme of Living" (*London Journal,* pp. 335–37) gives an excellent sense of the cost of living per year for a gentleman in the early 1760s:

Lodging	£ 50
Dinner	18
Breakfast	9 (eating in his room, with his own [locked] chest of tea and sugar)
Candles	6 (wax)
Coals	7 (7 ms./year, with fire only in the dining room)
Washing	6
Shoe cleaning	1
Clothes	50
Stockings and shoes	10
Total	£157

As a point of comparison, a poor family of six might spend £5 a year on clothes. They would not be troubled by such expenses of Boswell's as a suit of clean linens each day (£7/year), the dressing of one's hair on a daily or near-daily basis (£6/year), or the wiping of one's shoes at least once a day (£1/year). Boswell's budget allowed a remainder of £43, which would be used for "coach-hire, diversion, and the tavern, which I will find a very slight allowance." It is a good bit more than Johnson's £30 a year budget, but Johnson did not always feel the stress of poverty. For example, in his diary (*Diaries, Prayers, and Annals,* pp. 141–42) he lists some items purchased in 1771. He paid £4 for four large tablecloths, £7 for a teapot, and £10 for a coffee-pot. To speak of the cost of living in Johnson's London is to speak of a broad spectrum of activity, even within the experience of a single individual.

III. Pastimes and Pleasures

One does not tire of London unless one is tired of living, Johnson argued. "London" is synonymous with entertainment and diversion—in our own time and certainly no less so in Johnson's time. Some entertainments were genteel, some brutal, and some zany, but most were available to anyone with a small amount of discretionary income, and many were free. The attractions offered by London are too numerous to describe, but we can attempt to give some sense of the types of activities in which a Londoner or a traveler to London might indulge.

There were numerous attractions for visitors. London shops have already been discussed; they were as popular with travelers then as they are now. In addition to other sights already mentioned in the first chapter there was the British Museum, built at mid-century around the collection of Sir Hans Sloane, and of course the Tower of London. The museum's hours made it less accessible than it is now, but it grew steadily, for Sloane's collection was supplemented by the acquisition of the Harleian manuscripts and the royal library of George II. (The Elgin Marbles, the Rosetta Stone, and other famous acquisitions would come later.) The Tower's principal attraction was probably not its jewels, arms, and weapons, but its menagerie, which had different denizens at different times: lions, leopards, birds, bears, hyenas, and an occasional elephant. Saussure found ten lions, a panther, two tigers, four leopards, "a quantity of curious birds," and what the keeper called a "Tigerman," a "very big monkey . . . with a small white beard" which had come from Sumatra (*A Foreign View of England*, pp. 85–86). Kielmansegge found eagles, a horned owl, and lions "so tame that you can touch them with perfect safety" (*Diary of a Journey*

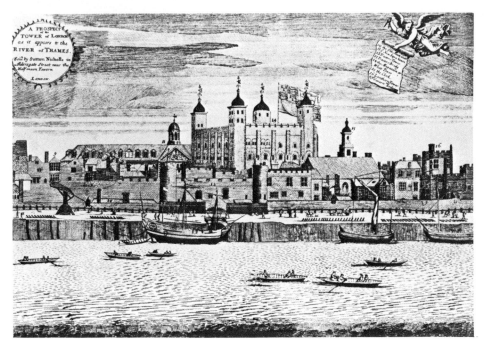

The Tower of London.

to England, p. 182). Archenholz described the social ambiance of the Tower: "The Tower is not a horrible prison, like the Bastile; it rather resembles a little town, abounding with tradesmen and artizans of every kind. A prodigious number of people reside there, and the apartments are very commodious" (*A Picture of England,* p. 56). Executions occurred on Tower Hill, and the Tower also contained the Mint, but surely one of its more curious attractions was the statue of Henry VIII. Saussure describes it teasingly: "He is represented standing in his royal robes, with a sceptre in his hand, and this is said to be a good likeness of this celebrated king. If you press a spot on the floor with your feet, you will see something surprising with regard to this figure; but I will not say more, and leave you to guess what it is" (*A Foreign View of England,* p. 88). The dummy's codpiece was overstuffed and lined with red velvet. It is said that women stuck pins in the codpiece believing that those who did so would never be barren. The mechanized operation which Saussure stops short of describing probably concerned the codpiece.

The theatre was of great importance to the eighteenth century. Covent Garden drew over 14,000 patrons a week in 1732, over 22,000 in 1762. Between 1700 and 1750, 1,095 new plays were produced; between 1750 and 1800, 2,117. Drury Lane's box office potential was £354 per performance in 1762. Its new theatre in 1792 seated 3,611 and was built at a cost of £150,000 (Plumb, *The Commercialisation of Leisure in Eighteenth-Century England,* p. 12). Opera offered competition to native English drama, but it could prove hazardous, because opera lovers wishing to follow the book would take candles with them to the theatre. Besides the risk of fire there was the less serious but no less real danger of damaging hand-tailored clothes with candle grease.

A well-known entertainment was the visiting of Bedlam hospital to view its insane patients. Both Johnson and Boswell went there. It had been an attraction as early as 1609, and though the practice of exploiting mental illness was criticized, the governors could point to £400 a year in admissions receipts plus publicity which might attract grants and bequests. Ned Ward found prostitutes and pickpockets there in numbers, as well as people selling nuts, beer, fruit, and cheesecakes (Altick, *The Shows of London,* pp. 44–45). Saussure reported the hospital to be frequented by members of the lower classes. He also found a porter at the exit, expecting a penny tip but refusing to give change if he received more.

Crowds in the streets amused themselves by, among other things, pelting those unfortunates locked in the pillory. They threw dirt, rotten eggs and vegetables, dead dogs and cats, trash, and ordure. In some cases they threw bricks and pieces of jagged metal. Time in the pillory, depending on the person and the offense, could be tantamount to a sentence of death. Mother Needham, the infamous bawd, died as a result of time spent in the pillory.

The crowd was not shy. They freely ridiculed passersby and

Drury Lane Theatre. Note the sedan chair, private coach, and wheelbarrow vendor.

Northeast corner, the Great Piazza, Covent Garden. At the end is the Shakespeare's Head Tavern; entrance to the theatre was to the left of the tavern.

sometimes with an intensity which would lead to temporary or even permanent exile. Women with outlandish clothes and hair styles were hooted away from theatres, and there are accounts of individuals being held up as laughingstocks to such an extent that they were forced to leave their district or village. Public executions will be discussed later, but their importance as a social event marked by both rituals and histrionics should be kept in mind in the present context.

The Thames bridges were popular for walks, for in addition to the view they afforded, they also offered a modicum of fresh air. Some preferred the Pall Mall promenade, which was strewn with sea shells that had been crushed by a roller. Both Hyde Park and St. James's were stocked with deer. One of the St. James's attractions was warm milk served directly from the

Bedlam Hospital, Moorfields.

cow. Although such milk might contain unpalatable substances such as blood, it was safer than the unrefrigerated milk found elsewhere and was not adulterated, a constant concern with eighteenth-century food, one to which we will return later.

The city's fairs were extremely popular. Fairs lasted from two to six weeks and featured, among other things, booths, wire walkers and rope-dancers, sideshows, acrobats, puppets, and sometimes wild animals. The world of the fair is captured nicely in Hogarth's portrayal of Southwark Fair; May Fair and Bartholomew Fair were also particularly noteworthy. In severe winters the frozen Thames would be the site of frost fairs. Many would come to see the booths or to skate, but another attraction, one still popular today, suggests that the eighteenth-century's assumption that human nature does not change is accurate. That attraction was the opportunity to see one's name in print. People set up print shops on the Thames and printed statements with the purchaser's name and the appropriate date (for example, "John Smith stood on the Thames on January 5, 1755"). For one line of printing the purchaser paid 6d.

St. James's Park.

London fairs could be raucous and, like most public gatherings, fruitful grounds for petty thieves and prostitutes. Coffeehouses were more subdued. They remain an inseparable part of our image of the eighteenth century and for good reason. Prior to the death of Queen Anne in 1714, there were approximately 3,000 coffeehouses in London. They were located throughout the city, but some catered to certain clienteles and were located accordingly. Merchants, for example, frequented coffeehouses near the Royal Exchange, while the booksellers' coffeehouses were near Paternoster Row. Men of means and fashion congregated near St. James's and Pall Mall, while wits and authors were to be found near Covent Garden or Temple Bar. According to Saussure, most of the coffeehouses were "not over clean or well furnished, owing to the quantity of people who resort to these places and because of the smoke, which would quickly destroy good furniture." Their chief attraction, he continued, was the presence there of newspapers: "All Englishmen are great newsmongers. Workmen habitually begin the day by going to coffee-rooms in order to read the latest news. I have often seen shoeblacks and other persons of

Hogarth: Southwark Fair.

that class club together to purchase a farthing paper" (*A Foreign View of England,* pp. 161–62).

To a great extent the club tradition emerged from the coffeehouse. Subscription rooms were reserved for particular groups; private clubs were formed which excluded outsiders. On some occasions the clubs expanded and absorbed the entire coffeehouse building, taking over the premises. Another type of society of considerable historical importance but less familiar to modern students of the eighteenth century is the freemasons' lodge. Archenholz, writing late in the century, said that there were 206 lodges in London alone.

Taverns provided food and drink and the opportunity to socialize. They offered rooms for private dining and, in some cases, were the setting for debates and lectures, frequently on

Thames frost fair.

moral or literary topics. Thus, while one set of tavern-goers might seek pints of porter, another group sought lectures on Shakespeare. Addison's twofold division of his reading audience was equally applicable to entertainment seekers:

> I may cast my Readers under two general Divisions, the *Mercurial* and the *Saturnine*. The first are the gay part of my Disciples, who require Speculations of Wit and Humour; the others are those of a more solemn and sober Turn, who find no Pleasure but in Papers of Morality and sound Sense; the former call every thing that is Serious Stupid. The latter look upon every thing as Impertinent that is Ludicrous. Were I always Grave one half of my Readers would fall off from me: Were I always Merry I should lose the other. I make it therefore my endeavour to find out Entertainments of both kinds. [*Spectator* 179]

Entertainments of both kinds were found in the streets as well as in the pages of the *Spectator*. While some busily argued affairs of state and raised questions concerning the economic well-being of the country, their fellow citizens might be watching a whistling match or grinning match (with the contestants framed by horse collars). One of Addison's correspondents (*Spectator* 179) reports on a yawning contest. The prize for the widest, most natural, and most yawn-inspiring yawn was a Cheshire cheese. While the sedentary might play chess, draughts, or backgammon, others might engage in smoking contests or hot hasty-pudding eating contests. There were contests in which the object was to catch a soaped pig, and familiar children's games such as leapfrog, hopscotch, marbles, and tops. Older brothers and sisters might be found disporting themselves in cemeteries—quiet, secluded locales which offered privacy and the opportunity for sexual intimacy. Then as now, cricket was popular. In writing to his family Saussure says of cricket, "I will not attempt to describe this game to you, it is too complicated" (*A Foreign View of England*, p. 295).

Hunting and fishing were favorite pursuits for Londoners who had ready access to the countryside. Angling was a common pastime. A rod was sometimes fashioned of spliced twigs, with a line made of horse hair. Baits included the eyes and spawn of fish and such substances as cow's brain. Scotland, a favorite spot for anglers, was not overfished. Large salmon and large perch, for example, were regularly taken there.

Hunting was the province of the gentleman. No one was allowed to kill game except owners of land worth £100 a year or lessees of land worth £150 a year. They were not restricted to their own property. They roamed freely unless warned off by a landowner or gamekeeper. Lands were sometimes guarded by spring guns or mantraps, and poison was sometimes laid for hunting dogs. Before the eighteenth century those living near forests could have hunting dogs only if they had been "lawed," that is, had three foreclaws chopped off so that they were too lame to chase deer. This was an archaic practice, but if gamekeepers found dogs hunting on their masters' property in the eighteenth century, they would not hesitate to destroy them. The struggle for survival, and for very valuable venison, con-

A coffeehouse.

tinued, however, with some setting razors in thickets so that deer would lame themselves and could be taken off by the poachers. The struggle between the gentleman hunter and starving rural poor is described in E. P. Thompson's *Whigs and Hunters.*

London offered darker pursuits. Opium was readily available. George Psalmanazar, Johnson's friend, was addicted to opium, and Johnson's wife used it. When we think of eighteenth-century drugs, we think first of alcohol (in the form of gin), but the opium which we associate with the Romantics was also available to their predecessors. In the eighteenth century some sniffed ether; ether "frolics" were popular.

In addition to the use of drugs, Londoners (and their country counterparts) enjoyed an array of bloodsports. Some were particular favorites of the lower classes; others had a broader appeal. Some bloodsports were practiced without regard to season or time (cockfighting, for example); others were associated with particular days. Throwing at cocks, for example, took place on Shrove Tuesday. The cock was tied to a stake by a cord, perhaps four to five feet in length. Competitors stood approximately twenty yards away and tried to knock the bird down by throwing a cudgel or broom stick at it. If the contestant succeeded in knocking the bird down, he had to pick it up before it rose. If he did so the cock was his. In some communities the cocks which managed to escape ("fugees") were the perquisite of the schoolmaster; those which were killed were given to the usher. When cock throwing was abolished in schools, "cock pennies" were given to undermasters in lieu of the bird's carcass. The fee for throwing at the cock was generally 2d. for three throws. If a bird was lamed, it was not uncommon to see it propped up with sticks and the contest continued. In some places the bird was put in a pot with head and tail exposed and suspended twelve to fourteen feet in the air. The person able to break the pot received a prize. When throwing at cocks was abolished, toy cocks with lead stands were substituted. Saussure observed a bout of cock throwing and described the "short, heavy wooden" clubs which were used. He cautions innocent passersby that "it is even dangerous on those days to go near any one of those places where this diversion is being held; so many clubs are thrown about that you run a risk of receiving one on your head" (*A Foreign View of England,* p. 294).

The baiting of fierce animals was very popular. Bulls were the most common victims, and they were generally baited in a tavern yard, a marketplace, or nearby field. The bull was tethered to an iron ring attached to a stake, with about fifteen feet of line. The dogs were held by their ears and then released one at a time. The dog attempted to seize the bull by the muzzle, the dewlap, or whatever else was accessible. The bull, on the other hand, tried to toss the dog so that his fall would break his neck. The crowd stood by, using poles to try to break the dog's fall (poles were held in parallel, so that the dog would slide down them). In some districts and communities, bull baiting was so popular that butchers could be assessed fines if they slaughtered bulls before they had been baited.

Bear baiting was popular but rarer because there were fewer bears. The bear attempted to defend himself against the dogs by either buffeting them or, if the dogs had attached themselves to him, by rolling on them. Badger baiting was more common. The badger was originally called the "grey"—hence greyhounds. He was allowed to run into a hole while the spectators bet on the number of times the dog would be able to draw him out within a given period of time. It was not uncommon for a badger to kill or maim a half dozen dogs before succumbing. There are also references to ass baiting, panther baiting, and otter baiting (otters were frequently hunted). Many of these practices declined in the eighteenth century, sometimes under force of law. Cock throwing would be found only in isolated instances in the nineteenth century, though bull baiting was still occurring as late as 1840.

Some activities might be considered a part of "normal" childhood behavior. For example, children placed snail shells against one another and pressed until one, or sometimes both, shells broke. This was called "conquering." Children used fly guns to shoot at flies and put threads through mayflies, drawing them back when the insects attempted to escape. Other activities, however, can only be seen as patently brutal. "Goose riders," for example, hung a goose by the legs from a tree bough or attached it to a rope stretched between two poles. The bird's neck was greased and the competitors, riding beneath it at top speed, attempted to pull off the goose's head. In some cases owls were tied to the backs of ducks. When the duck dove, the owl nearly drowned. He hooted and the frightened duck dove again. The process then repeated in cycle. Johnson's compassionate comments on cruelty to animals and on vivisection should be seen in the context of eighteenth-century practice, where they take on additional force.

Some bloodsports were localized, others institutional. The bull-running at Tutbury in Staffordshire was renowned for its frenzy. Pepper was put in the bull's nose to exacerbate the situation. The ram hunt at Eton (abolished in 1747) was held at the beginning of August at electiontide. The boys hunted a ram through the streets of the town, armed with clubs.

Like badger baiting, dog fighting was a secondary amusement. Cock fighting is a more familiar eighteenth-century practice, partly because it is described by Boswell and depicted by Hogarth. The bouts, or mains, were overlaid with a great deal of ritual. The care and feeding of a fighting cock was a matter of serious study. White corn or white bread were recommended as feed. Cotton (*The Compleat Gamester,* in Hartmann, *Games and Gamesters,* p. 105) recommends toasting the white bread and steeping it in drink or human urine, "which will both scoure and cool them inwardly." He advises licking the rooster's eyes and head and treating his wounds with warm urine. Fighting roosters fought with clipped wings and tails, with filed beaks and spurs. In some cases the spurs were very long. A rooster could catch himself on his own spurs and break his legs. Fights were held both at actual cockpits and in inns specially fitted for the mains. Fights lasted for hours, with feverish betting and an incessant din. The Welsh main, a special favorite, involved an elimination match, usually with thirty-two cocks, only one of which would survive. At the Royal Cockpit, Westminster (illustrated by Hogarth), defaulters on bets were put in baskets and suspended from the ceiling.

Hogarth: The Cockpit. One can see the shadow of a figure suspended in the basket.

Boswell describes his experience there in December 1762:

> I then went to the Cockpit, which is a circular room in the
> middle of which the cocks fight. It is seated round with rows
> gradually rising. The pit and the seats are all covered with
> mat. The cocks, nicely cut and dressed and armed with silver
> heels, are set down and fight with amazing bitterness and
> resolution. Some of them were quickly dispatched. One pair
> fought three quarters of an hour. The uproar and noise of
> betting is prodigious. A great deal of money made a very
> quick circulation from hand to hand. There was a number of
> professed gamblers there. An old cunning dog whose face I
> had seen at Newmarket sat by me a while. I told him I knew

nothing of the matter. 'Sir,' said he, 'you have as good a chance as anybody.' He thought I would be a good subject for him. I was young-like. But he found himself balked. I was shocked to see the distraction and anxiety of the betters. I was sorry for the poor cocks. I looked round to see if any of the spectators pitied them when mangled and torn in a most cruel manner, but I could not observe the smallest relenting sign in any countenance. I was therefore not ill pleased to see them endure mental torment. [*London Journal*, p. 87]

There were fights between humans also. Bare-fisted boxing matches of as many as thirty rounds were not uncommon. (Johnson's uncle Andrew was a celebrated boxer and wrestler. He held the ring at Smithfield against all comers for an entire year and, according to Mrs. Piozzi, instructed his nephew Sam in boxing techniques.) There were female boxers as well. It is said that they were sometimes forced to hold coins in their hands while boxing. This would deter the pulling of hair because the coin would be risked in the process. Grosley (*A Tour to London*, 1:59) observed a boxing match in Holborn between a man and a woman.

Cudgeling, backsword, and singlestick were forms of stick dueling. The object was to draw blood—"to break a head." An ad in 1753 read, "No Head to be deemed broke unless the Blood runs an Inch" (Malcolmson, *Popular Recreations in English Society*, p. 43). To draw blood the contestants aimed for the head, the nose, and the teeth. Very often a contestant (including the women) would be cut, retire to be sewn up, take a glass of spirits, and then return to the battle.

For many, the simplest pastime and quickest pleasure came from liquor. The image of the hard-drinking eighteenth-century gentleman is a bit exaggerated. The four-bottle squire drank large quantities, to be sure. He might take a claret, burgundy, or Rhenish with dinner, a port or Madeira with dessert. He avoided water, not because of alcohol addiction, but because the water was unsafe. Yet when he drank large amounts of wine (which he did frequently), he drank over a long period of time. The toasts and talk which followed dinner

The virtues of punch, a late-eighteenth-century cartoon by Gillray.

would go on for hours. Wine might be drunk in quantity without producing drunkenness.

Port was popular because it was cheaper than claret. Trade with Portugal was less tax-ridden than trade with France, although many Jacobites would drink French wines as a political statement. Port, which was more like a burgundy in the eighteenth century, had supplanted sack, the seventeenth century's preference. Punch, another eighteenth-century favorite, was, in Saussure's words, "composed of sour and sweet, of strong and of weak" (*A Foreign View of England*, p. 160). It would consist of such ingredients as lemons, oranges, sugar, and brandy. "Bishop" would generally include hot port, sugar, nutmeg, and a roasted orange, "negus" hot water, wine, lemon, and sugar. Possets consisted of milk curdled with wine, egg yolks, and cinnamon or nutmeg. Syllabubs included new milk warm from the cow. A Somerset syllabub would add port or sherry to the milk, which would then be covered with cream. Other syllabubs might consist of nothing more than one-third glass of wine topped off with the warm milk. The rich might have their own ice houses. In London ice would be purchased from the fishmongers.

The poor drank beer and, for a time, gin. From approximately 1720 to 1750 gin was drunk in sufficient quantity to term the period that of the "gin madness." In the 1730s and 1740s there were at least six thousand places in London where gin could be purchased, and that figure does not include the stalls and barrows from which it would also be sold. In some districts every fifth house contained an outlet for gin, and liquor was also freely sold in prisons. Final production neared nine million gallons per year. In 1751 an act was passed which increased the duty on spirits and denied distillers, chandlers, and grocers the right to retail. The problem did not disappear immediately, but amelioration began. In his *Enquiry into the Causes of the late Increase of Robbers* Fielding had estimated that gin was the principal sustenance of more than 100,000 people in London alone (p. 18). The ads offering drunkenness for a penny, dead drunkenness for a tuppence, frequently included the availability of a straw-covered cellar for recuperation as well.

The cheapness of gin had resulted from conscious economic policy. Distilling received special favors from the government, for in times of plenty grain could be used for the production of spirits, a great boon for the agricultural economy. The presence of the distiller, existing in a kind of partnership with the landowner, removed fears of overproduction. The poor constituted a ready market for the product. The social costs—in crime, illegitimacy, absenteeism, and broken health—were enormous. In addition, the presence of stills in urban areas like London constituted a serious fire hazard. Fielding refers to a report from Welch, the high constable of Holborn, on some of the effects of the gin madness:

In the Parish of St. *Giles*'s there are great Numbers of Houses set apart for the Reception of idle Persons and Vagabonds, who have their Lodgings there for Twopence a Night: . . . in the above Parish, and in St. *George, Bloomsbury*, one Woman alone occupies seven of these Houses, all properly accommodated with miserable Beds from the Cellar to the Garret, for such Twopenny Lodgers: That in these Beds, several of which are in the same Room, Men and Women, often Strangers to each other, lie promiscuously, the Price of a double Bed being no more than Threepence, as an Encouragement to them to lie together: . . . as these Places are thus adapted to Whoredom, so are they no less provided for Drunkenness, Gin being sold in them all at a Penny a Quartern; so that the smallest Sum of Money serves for Intoxication: . . . in the Execution of Search-Warrants, Mr. *Welch* rarely finds less than Twenty of these Houses open for the Receipt of all Comers at the latest Hours: . . . in one of these Houses, and that not a large one, he hath numbered 58 Persons of both Sexes, the Stench of whom was so intolerable that it compelled him in a very short time to quit the Place. [*An Enquiry into the Causes of the late Increase of Robbers*, pp. 91–92]

Early in the century per capita consumption of gin approached six gallons per year, and gin was not the only drink of the London poor. Cider was also drunk, although it was popular chiefly in the western counties and in Herefordshire and Kent. Cider could be dangerous, for lead pipes and vessels were sometimes used in its preparation and storage. (The leather bottles in which beer and cider were sometimes kept must have been extremely difficult to clean.) Beer was consumed in great quantities. In 1786 the principal brewers made 1,178,856 barrels of strong beer. There was also, of course, small beer and home brew. Thrale's was brewing over 100,000 barrels; Whitbread, 150,000. Brewing was one of Southwark's principal industries; the district had long been known for inns and eating houses which brewed their own beer. Benjamin Franklin's fellow printers took a pint before breakfast, a pint with their bread and cheese breakfast, a pint between breakfast and dinner, one with dinner, one at 6:00, and one upon finishing work—in other words, at least three quarts a day. The pensioners at Greenwich Hospital were each allotted fourteen quarts per week. Obviously, Thrale dealt in a product that was in demand.

Drinking feats were the subject of much interest. Two friends of Sir Philip Francis drank ten bottles of champagne at a sitting. Dr. John Campbell is reported to have consumed thirteen bottles of port. It was said that some laborers in Gloucestershire could swallow a gallon of cider in a single drink. Kronenberger writes that Porson the classicist would drink ink if there was nothing else available (*Kings & Desperate Men,* p. 253).

If the century often exhibited excess in its drinking, its approach to gambling or "gaming," as it was termed, bordered on the obsessive. The politician Charles James Fox, for example, had debts of £140,000 at the age of twenty-four. He would often play for twenty-four hours at a sitting, sometimes losing £500 an hour. One night the gamesters at the Cocoa Tree lost £180,000. The Duke of Devonshire lost Leicester Abbey at the gaming table. As a way of recovering their money, the creditors of a notorious cheat would let him out of debtors' prison whenever Chesterfield (who was both intemperate and unlucky) was in London (Kronenberger, *Kings & Desperate Men,* p. 252). The story of Lord Stavordale, recounted by Horace Walpole, is a famous one. Walpole lamented the losses which young gamesters were prepared to sustain. A loss of five, ten, or even fifteen thousand pounds was not uncommon in an evening at White's. Stavordale, not yet twenty-one years of age, lost £11,000 one evening and recovered it in a single play. After swearing a strong oath, he exclaimed, "Now, if I had been playing *deep,* I might have won millions."

Men and women played cards, but many favored dice, particularly when the game was hazard, a game in which many fortunes had been won and lost. When the floor of Middle Temple Hall was removed in 1764, the workmen found nearly a hundred pairs of dice which had fallen through the cracks between the boards (Hartmann, *Games and Gamesters,* xii). Cockfight betting has already been mentioned. Kielmansegge describes his experience at a cockpit: "No one who has not seen such a sight can conceive the uproar by which it is accompanied, as everybody at the same time offers and accepts bets. You cannot hear yourself speak, and it is impossible for those who are betting to understand one another, therefore the men who take the bets, which are seldom even, but odds, such as 5 to 4, or 21 to 20, make themselves understood to the layers of the bets by signs" (*Diary of a Journey to England,* p. 242).

Gaming could unite the age's gentility and brutality in a single moment. The *Biographia Dramatica* (2:358) recounts the story of Baron Newman, a notorious gambler who achieved part of his fame while playing at picquet. One of his opponents, suspecting that Newman had palmed a card, took a fork, jabbed it through the baron's hand and into the table, and said, "Monsieur Baron, if you have not a card under your hand, I beg your pardon." A card was there, and like the baron's hand, it was pierced by the fork.

State lotteries were common after the late 1770s. They had been used earlier from time to time as governmental financial expedients. Such gaming could bring ruin and misery, but it was not as picturesque or zany as some of the other practices in which the century indulged. For example, it was not uncommon to find bets being placed on whether or not a boxer or an accident victim would recover from his injuries. In such cases physicians would not be allowed to attend the injured party, lest the bet be affected. Archenholz writes of lice races: "The passion for betting is so very strong among the English, that the pensioners of Chelsea and Greenwich Hospitals, being unable to indulge themselves in either horse or ass-races, have been known to wager on the *speed* of vermin" (*A Picture of England,* p. 250). The contestants would be drawn from the bettors' bodies. Turkeys and geese were also raced, but partly for the curiosity of it; horse racing was a much more serious business. One of Eclipse's colts sold for 1,000 guineas down, 500 more if his first race were won. The owner of Eclipse was once offered 11,000 guineas for his horse.

The Chevalier d'Éon. An accomplished duellist, d'Éon duelled in both men's and women's attire.

One of the more interesting occasions for gaming was that presented by the hermaphroditic Chevalier d'Éon de Beaumont. D'Éon was a spy for Louis XV. Baptized male, he was called Geneviève as well as Charles. Once judged to be female, a postmortem claimed that he was male. In England bets on his actual sex amounted to £120,000. In the mid-1770s a man wagered that he could dive at Plymouth in a submarine-like ship, stay under water for twelve hours, and then have the ship (with him in it) surface. He failed and drowned. Two months later there was talk of raising the vessel. Wagers were laid at two Pall Mall coffeehouses concerning the position in which the man's body would be found (Hampden, *An Eighteenth-Century Journal*, pp. 83–84 and 92*n*).

Gaming, particularly "deep" gaming, was usually an upper-class activity. But prostitution, particularly associated with the eighteenth century, brought together rich and poor. Grosley described the prostitutes of London as more numerous than those in Paris, and as taking greater liberty and demonstrating more effrontery than those in Rome (*A Tour to London,* 1:55). They were frequently seen in groups of five or six, accosting passersby with invitations. It was not uncommon for London prostitutes to take hold of potential customers in carnal fashion. For Baretti, the Thrales' tutor, such an incident had led to a charge of murder. He was "assailed in the grossest manner possible by a woman of the town," struck her, and was set upon by three men. He defended himself with a knife, stabbed two of his attackers, and was tried and finally acquitted (*Life,* 2:96–98 and 97*n*).

Prostitutes were especially seen at Charing Cross, along the Strand, in Fleet Street, and in the vicinity of Covent Garden. Under the piazza in Covent Garden one could purchase Harris' *New Atlantis,* a guidebook to London prostitutes, detailing addresses, physical characteristics, and specialties. Archenholz claimed that there were eight thousand copies sold annually (*A Picture of England,* p. 197). In Covent Garden trysts might be set up in the back rooms of taverns, in lodging houses, or in bagnios. Genuine bagnios—"hummums"—were for taking Turkish baths. Ladies and gentlemen were admitted on separate days, with back entrances for the shy, and the opportunity to rent a bath for yourself if you were very shy. Brothels were located in various places, but concentrated at Covent Garden, Charing Cross, on the south side of Fleet Street, at the back of Bridewell, and in Alsatia. There were specialized brothels—for homosexuals and for sadomasochists, for example, and at least one all-black brothel. Flagellation was common; indeed, there were clubs for such purposes. In plate 3 of *A Harlot's Progress* Hogarth shows a bundle of birch rods on the wall above the bed. The London gentleman might indulge in more "romantic" activities. For example, anchored opposite Somerset House was the *Folly,* a kind of brothel afloat. On the first floor were musicians, "water-nymphs," and "tritons"; on the second floor, small apartments for trysts. The *Folly* introduced a dimension of fantasy into what was often a fairly direct business transaction.

As was indicated earlier, the prostitutes were often very

HARRIS's LIST

OF

Covent-Garden Ladies:

OR

.MAN OF PLEASURE's

KALENDAR,

For the YEAR 1773.

CONTAINING

An exact Description of the most celebrated Ladies of Pleasure who frequent COVENT-
GARDEN, and other parts of this Metropolis.

THE SECOND EDITION.

LONDON.

Printed for H. RANGER, Temple Exchange
Passage, Fleet-Street.

M DCC LXXIII.

(Left) *Harris's guide to London prostitutes.*
(Above) *The* Folly.

young, some even under the age of ten. Pennant describes a group of them he saw at Bridewell:

> The first time I visited the place, there was not a single male prisoner, and about twenty female. They were confined on a ground-floor, and employed in beating of hemp. When the door was opened by the keeper, they ran towards it like so many hounds in kennel; and presented a most moving sight: about twenty young creatures, the eldest not exceeding sixteen, many of them with angelic faces, divested of every angelic expression; and featured with impudence, impenitency, and profligacy; and cloathed in the silken tatters of squalid finery. [*Some Account of London,* p. 219]

A 1758 survey of twenty-five prostitutes in and around the Strand revealed a median age of eighteen. The median age for beginning as prostitutes was sixteen and a half, with seven girls beginning at the age of fourteen or younger. Seventeen of the twenty-five were orphans; another five had been abandoned. Most had severe venereal disease. None were active after the age of twenty-two or for longer than six years. Most were able to prostitute themselves for only one to three years (Stone, *The Family, Sex, and Marriage,* p. 618). We must remember that in addition to perhaps 50,000 prostitutes there were kept mistresses and stylish courtesans like Kitty Fisher, who could, it is said, command 100 guineas a night. For them life was far less severe. But for the young girls and women in the streets the situation was far from romantic. They were poor, ignorant, and defenseless, often from the country, often orphaned or abandoned.

Archenholz (*A Picture of England,* p. 196) claimed that the prostitutes were one of the keys to London's economy, in that they bought fine clothes, frequented the theatre and various public places, and thus attracted young men there. That may well be true, but the economy to which they contributed dealt harshly with them, though not always with their bawds. The "women of the town" were often children of the town, and their lives were wretched. Johnson's charity on their behalf—caring for them and nursing them back to health—is well-known.

One place where one would very likely encounter prostitutes was the London pleasure garden. There were perhaps sixty or seventy such places during the eighteenth century. Many were short-lived and very modest, consisting only of a tea garden or perhaps a tavern and bowling green. The grand gardens were Vauxhall and Ranelagh. Vauxhall had a fairytale atmosphere which contrasted with the elegance of Ranelagh. While Vauxhall was designed as a summer resort, Ranelagh, with its 185-foot-wide rotunda and huge central fireplace, was an all-weather structure. Ranelagh was a place to take tea, to see and to be seen. Johnson said of Ranelagh that the "*coup d'oeil* was the finest thing he had ever seen" (*Life,* 2:168), but Vauxhall finally proved more popular.

Vauxhall had been founded by Jonathan Tyers, father of

Vauxhall at mid-century.

Thomas Tyers, Johnson's friend, who for a time served as its joint manager. Ranelagh was in Chelsea; Vauxhall, on the south bank of the river, west of Westminster Bridge. Vauxhall had a Chinese temple, hermit's cottage, and smugglers' cave, a lovers' walk and musical bushes where an orchestra hidden underground played fairy music. (The musicians complained of damage to their instruments from the dampness.) There were also clockwork mechanisms, trompe l'oeil paintings, and very high prices for refreshments. The ham was legendary for its thinness. The price of food contrasted with the relatively egalitarian entrance fee of 1 s. What money one had would have to be protected from the pickpockets who naturally frequented the pleasure gardens. The very lucky traveler might find pleasanter surprises. A visitor to Ranelagh in 1764, for example, might have heard a concert on harpsichord and organ performed for charity by an eight-year-old composer named Mozart.

The Ranelagh rotunda, with its dining tables and blazing fire.

More polite pursuits: an Academy exhibition. Note the manner in which works were displayed.

Johnson was intrigued by the attractions and shows which London offered and visited many of them, often with Boswell. London's shows were often interesting, sometimes tasteless and crude, sometimes complex and sophisticated. It goes without saying that the shows catered to all tastes. The scientifically oriented would enjoy balloon ascents, automata, magic lantern shows, and de Loutherbourg's Eidophusikon, an invention which brought together the clockwork picture, transparency, and use of concentrated lighting. Moving, three-dimensional models, the use of light and shade, and the manipulation of perspective were used to create scenes such as Niagara Falls or the raising of Pandemonium for the spectator (see Altick, *The Shows of London*, pp. 119–24). One of the most frequent spectators was Sir Joshua Reynolds.

There were waxworks such as Mrs. Salmon's in Fleet Street, near the entrance to the Temple. Waxworks often included representations of royalty, as well as biblical characters and heroes and villains from legends and from history. Rosamond Bayne-Powell writes that both Johnson and Wilkes were repre-

The Eidophusikon.

sented at Mrs. Salmon's (*The English Child in the Eighteenth Century,* p. 188).

There were other familiar shows: fireworks, peepshows, mountebanks, fire eaters, trick horse riders, and fortune-tellers. Sideshows included midgets, giants, what would later be called "Siamese" twins, hermaphrodites, and "posture makers," generally people who were double jointed and who contorted themselves in ways designed to surprise, amuse, and disgust the audience. Savages (both noble and otherwise) were exhibited. Cripples would perform stunts. For example, an armless man might comb his hair and shave himself with his foot. The best was a twenty-nine-inch dwarf named Mathew Buchinger. Lacking both hands and legs, Buchinger could still play the oboe, write and draw with a pen, and dance a hornpipe in Highland dress (Altick, *The Shows of London,* p. 43). Voice impressionists imitated birds, domestic animals, and musical instruments. There were eaters of raw flesh and eaters

Rowlandson: The "learned pig."

of stones, a rope dancer who performed with children tied to his feet, a Scotsman who broke glasses by shouting at them, and displays of feats of miniaturization—for example, carved cherry stones. On his way to Westminster Bridge, Kielmansegge saw an enormous pig, so fat that it could not move. It had been brought to London to be exhibited (*Diary of a Journey to England,* p. 189). Kalm was intrigued with a snake handler:

> We saw today as well as on the previous days a common man clad in rags, who had a large collection of living Vipers and snakes, which he went and carried about in the streets, to show to folk for money. He could handle them with his hands quite quietly, and without the snakes offering in the least to bite him. He had a bag in which he laid them, and when anyone gave him [a halfpence] he took them out with his hands, either one after another or also by the handfull, as many as he could hold. Often to awaken more astonishment,

Sedan chairs for hire in Charing Cross.

he stuffed either a viper or a snake whole into his mouth and kept his mouth shut for a little while, and then opened his mouth and let the snake crawl out of it. [*Kalm's Account of His Visit to England,* p. 38]

While the more polite might enjoy the museum at Don Saltero's Chelsea coffeehouse, there were attractions of a more sanguinary nature. Execution ropes used on the famous (or infamous) were exhibited; Cromwell's head made the rounds of London fairs and shows for years. In the case of a notable execution, the undertaker might exhibit the corpse for a time. Traitors' heads were piked above Temple Bar, and spyglasses were rented to those who wanted a better look at them. After the French Revolution a model of the guillotine was erected in the Haymarket, and life-size mannikins were decapitated. An enterprising dentist had his dead wife embalmed and displayed in a glass case. (He stopped the practice when he remarried.)

"Centaur," exhibited in London in the mid-eighteenth century.

Some of the shows were curious indeed. At Somerset House in 1701 a Dutch boy was exhibited who had Hebrew written on the irises of his eyes. Trained animals and birds were sometimes remarkable. Readers of Boswell are familiar with the so-called "learned pig" (*Life,* 4:373–74). Horses were often trained as well. Birds had been a favorite since Tudor times. One of the more striking feats performed by birds was the mock execution. Birds marched in ranks with toy guns, halted, and fired at one bird, who fell down and "died" on cue. At a given signal he revived, and the birds marched off together. Perhaps the most expensive of the attractions of London was "Dr." James Graham's Temple of Health in Adelphi Terrace. For 2 guineas admission one could receive lectures on sex and health. For £50 per night one could sleep in Graham's "celestial bed." The bed, said to have cost £10,000 to build and equip, was twelve by nine feet, had live birds and musical instruments, and a canopy supported by forty glass pillars. It was supposed to offer both pleasure and results, for the bed could be tilted after coition, presumably to aid conception. It was not a financial success (£2,000 per night in modern currency was a tad high apparently), and Graham turned to the mud bath business instead.

Many of the shows were set up on the streets or at fairs, but inns rented space to exhibitors, particularly the inns at Charing Cross, in the Strand, and in Fleet Street. During the two weeks of Bartholomew Fair one could drink, gamble, brawl, and stare at passers-by. The shows might include magicians, acrobats, wire walkers, mountebanks with nostrums, ballad singers, and religious fanatics, with pickpockets and prostitutes thrown into the bargain. At an inn in Charing Cross, one might see a talking centaur (a legless soldier or seaman attached to a stuffed, decapitated horse) or a living, breathing mermaid (a woman with a scaly tail attached). Johnson saw the full tide of human existence at Charing Cross, but there was much more there than coach traffic.

IV. Daily Routines
and Domestic Life

Individuals structure their lives in many ways and take these routines for granted. Foreign travelers immediately notice patterns of behavior that permanent residents never question. In Johnson's London the structure of the day varied markedly from rank to rank, and it is not too great a generalization to say that common residents of the same city lived in different temporal worlds as well as different financial ones. Johnson moved in different worlds at different points of his life. He knew the leisurely life of the gentleman, the hurried life of the tradesman, and the unceasing toil of the group which he termed the industrious poor. It is important to keep this experience in mind when we comment on Johnson's division of his own time, for Johnson's practice can easily be misinterpreted.

We tend to think of Johnson as being entrenched in a city from which he could not leave; departure from the city would constitute exile. Boswell writes that Johnson turned down a clerical post in Lincolnshire partly because "he would have thought himself an exile in any other place" (*Life*, 1:320). It would be silly to deny Johnson's love of the city, particularly its diversity and the ways in which it kept his mind in motion, but Johnson sometimes spoke of himself as an exile within the city. He wrote to Thomas Warton about his wife's death: "I have ever since seemed to myself broken off from mankind a kind of solitary wanderer in the wild of life, without any certain direction, or fixed point of view. A gloomy gazer on a World to which I have little relation" (*Letters*, 1:59). To Joseph Simpson he writes: "Whither I fly is Matter of no Importance. A Man unconnected is at home every-where, unless he may be said to be at home no where" (*Letters*, 1:127). This sense of loneliness and isolation might have resulted in part from a transient mood, and certainly the death of Johnson's wife contributed to it. Yet, in some important ways, Johnson was alone. He did not share the financial success and stature of Reynolds. He was not a politician, a man of business, a doctor, or a lawyer, like so many of his friends. As a professional writer he had colleagues but not peers. He was comfortable in the Thrale household, but his own family was elsewhere. This situation brought pain from time to time, but the pain was counterbalanced by freedom and mobility. He was not tied to London by land or family, but in some ways he could be more "at home" in London because he could move through such different areas of experience within it. London's inhabitants often moved in their separate circles. Johnson moved across them. Thus, while he was not, in some senses, "at home" there, it is still not inappropriate to consider Johnson the quintessential Londoner.

A fourteen- to fifteen-hour working day would not be uncommon for the working poor in the city. They might work from 5 or 6 A.M. until 8 or 9 P.M., completing what would nearly be a modern day's work before the wealthy had even awakened. The tradesman worked long hours as well. Handicraft trades had hours of 6 A.M. to 8 or 9 P.M., in some cases 5 A.M. to 9 P.M. A shopkeeper at mid-century would probably open at 7 A.M. and not close until 8 P.M. (and even later as the century progressed). In general there were few holidays. The work week was six days long, with breaks at Christmas, Easter, and Whitsuntide. Many also had holidays on the eight days during the year when there were hangings at Tyburn, and this partly as a warning against idleness and its wages.

While the poor might face tedium and drudgery, the shopkeeper at least experienced some variety in his day. He might, for example, rise at five, do some office work, take breakfast at eight, and work until ten-thirty, when he departed for the coffeehouse for news. He would return to the shop, take dinner at noon, leave for the Royal Exchange at one, and go to a coffeehouse to conduct business from three to four. He would then return to the shop and work for a time, after which he might return to the coffeehouse for recreation with friends.

His supper would be light, and he would retire about 9 P.M.

For the wealthy, the day was quite different. Archenholz writes that "the English live in a very remarkable manner. They rise late, and spend most of the morning, either in walking about town or sitting in the coffee-house" (*A Picture of England*, p. 199). Rochefoucauld was also surprised by the life of the Londoner: "The conduct of an Englishman's day in London leaves little time for work. He gets up at ten or eleven and has breakfast (always with tea). He then makes a tour of the town for about four hours until 5 o'clock, which is the dinner hour; at 9 o'clock in the evening he meets his friends in a tavern or a club and there the night is passed in play and drink; that is precisely how the day is spent" (*A Frenchman in England*, p. 19). There would be times, of course, when the fashionable Londoner would be at the theatre rather than the tavern or club. While the poor had already been working for five or six hours, the rich would breakfast at ten o'clock or a bit later. They would take dinner between five and seven and supper between ten and, at the latest, two o'clock—hours after the shopkeeper, tradesman, and the laboring poor had retired for the night. The trend in fashion was to hold later and later suppers as the century progressed.

Given this situation, it is difficult to generalize about Johnson's ordering of his life. While working on the *Dictionary* his hours must have been (for him) comparatively regular, and he must have risen earlier than he would later in life. There would be Monday and Friday *Rambler* deadlines and Tuesday evening meetings of the Ivy Lane Club. After completing the *Dictionary* he predictably (and deservedly) relaxed. Murphy reports his rising at 2 P.M. and spending the day receiving friends and writers. The Johnson that Boswell found was residing in Inner Temple Lane. The Gough Square experience was behind him. His pattern of life was described by the reader at the Temple Church, William Maxwell:

> His general mode of life, during my acquaintance, seemed to be pretty uniform. About twelve o'clock I commonly visited him, and frequently found him in bed, or declaiming

over his tea, which he drank very plentifully. He generally
had a levee of morning visitors, chiefly men of letters. . . .
He declaimed all the morning, then went to dinner at a
tavern, where he commonly staid late, and then drank his tea
at some friend's house, over which he loitered a great while,
but seldom took supper. I fancy he must have read and
wrote chiefly in the night, for I can scarcely recollect that he
ever refused going with me to a tavern, and he often went to
Ranelagh, which he deemed a place of innocent recreation.
[*Life*, 2:118–19]

This is the Johnson of the nineteenth century: the indolent
genius, holding court and taking tea, keeping his companions
up until all hours and indulging his clubable nature while
keeping his melancholy at arm's length. In point of fact, Johnson's life is not very different from the lives of his wealthy
fellow citizens. Late rising, late retiring, and lengthy socializing
were the rule and not the exception. Contemporaries were
surprised at his pattern of living because there seemed to be
little time available for study and writing, but the pattern itself
is in no way exceptional. With Johnson, particularly the Johnson of the *Prayers and Meditations,* there is an important religious dimension to the ordering of time. The injunctions
implicit in the parable of the talents reminded Johnson of his
responsibilities and resulted in resolutions to rise earlier and
order his time and activities more rigorously. His talents reminded him of the life from which he had been freed—that of
the poor—and his contacts with booksellers, printers, tradesmen, and shopkeepers reminded him of the manner in which
other lives were perforce ordered.

Certainly "intellectuals" would not have been expected to
lead lives of long hours and intense study. Thomas Campbell
writes in his diary: "A gownsman of Oxford thus painted the
fellows of All Souls—They lived so luxuriously & indolently
that they did nothing but clean their teeth all the morning &
pick them all the evening" (*Dr. Campbell's Diary of a Visit to
England,* p. 43). Rochefoucauld writes of a foppish clergyman
who took a Cambridge doctorate. He was asked whether the

The Royal Exchange.

sun turned round the earth or the earth round the sun: "Not knowing what to say and wanting to make some reply, he assumed an emphatic air and boldly exclaimed: 'Sometimes the one, sometimes the other'. This reply produced so much amusement that he was made a doctor on the strength of this piece of fatuous stupidity" (*A Frenchman in England*, p. 222). Part of the reason that Johnson's pattern of living would appear somewhat out of the ordinary was that he usually lived in the City. His wealthy, late-rising, late-retiring counterparts would generally be found in Westminster.

Up until now we have not drawn a distinction between the City and the metropolis of which it is a part, but the distinction is extremely important in a number of respects. From time to time Johnson lived outside the City, of course, but he was most comfortable within its confines, particularly in the area around

The Mansion House, home of the lord mayor of the City of London.

Fleet Street. Saussure found the City of London to be "almost entirely inhabited by merchants" (*A Foreign View of England,* p. 36), and the commercial tradition—of great political and economic importance before and during Johnson's time—continues today.

The City consists of the area within the original position of the city walls plus the liberties, or suburbs, beyond the walls. It occupies little over a single square mile (actually 677 acres), a very small part of the over 700 square miles of modern greater London. In the eighteenth century the City was governed by its lord mayor, over two dozen aldermen, two sheriffs, a recorder, and common council. Although there were twenty-nine guilds, the lord mayor could only be chosen from one of the twelve principal guilds: the Mercers, Grocers, Drapers, Fishmongers, Goldsmiths, Skinners, Merchant Taylors, Haberdashers, Salters, Ironmongers, Vintners, and Clothworkers.

The City is traditionally associated with commerce; Westminster, with the monarchy. There kings and queens are crowned and buried. Edward the Confessor made his palace

The Guildhall.

beside his abbey at Westminster, and British monarchs still go to the Abbey rather than to St. Paul's. William the Conqueror was crowned on Christmas Day in 1066 in the Abbey. During the Interregnum the City supported the Parliamentarians while Westminster remained Royalist. Today these lines are largely ceremonial, but in Johnson's time they were drawn more rigorously. The differences between Westminster and the City were immediately apparent to foreign travelers, including the differences in the division of time. Here is Moritz: "In Westminster the morning lasts until about four or five in the afternoon, when first they dine and then arrange their supper and bedtime accordingly. Breakfast is generally taken at ten in the morning. The farther you go from the Court towards the City, however, the more middle-class they become. There they dine usually at three o'clock, or in effect as soon as the business is over on 'Change" (*Journeys of a German in England*, p. 69).

The modern student of the eighteenth century is aware of

Whats Interregnum

Westminster Abbey.

the lines of rank which affected eighteenth-century social and economic life, but is not always aware of the fine distinctions which could be drawn or the manner in which the distinctions might be made. Wealth, title, and genealogy are readily apparent, as is occupation and the district in which one lived. Then as now, the rental of property would confer less distinction than its ownership. The eighteenth century would also inquire concerning the location of the property—that is, whether it sat on a square, in a row, a street, a place, or in a court or an alley. The floor or floors on which one resided would be very important as well. Deviations from predicted behavior would be more striking in a situation such as this. Thus, Johnson's daily routine would fit a Westminster pattern far more closely than a City pattern. Yet he very often resided in the City. His physical appearance was probably not out of the ordinary for his district and income, but his wealthy friends might be taken aback by the state of his dress. When *he* dressed in gold lace for the performance of *Irene,* his friends might well take notice of it, but the presence of gold lace at Drury Lane was hardly uncommon. In moving across economic and social lines, as his intellect, industry, personality, and sense of compassion permitted him to do, his behavior, dress, or pattern of living sometimes occasioned surprise, surprise which can easily be misinterpreted.

Among those activities which are central to the ordering of the day few are more important than the taking of food. Johnson's own diet and table manners are part and parcel of the nineteenth-century caricature of the man which we have inherited. Johnson's practice should be seen in its eighteenth-century context, and there again the question of rank intrudes.

The poor subsisted largely on bread, cheese, tea, and beer. There might be an occasional bit of meat, if it was cheap, and an occasional fish. The diet would vary from one part of the country to another. For example, oatmeal or potatoes would be seen more often in the North, where there might also be less meat and more milk. In the South, cottage gardens would produce cabbage, onions, and carrots for an occasional soup or stew.

The artisan would have bread, cheese, tea, and beer, but would also be able to afford some butter, meats, and vegetables. A country gentleman would have tea, coffee, or chocolate for breakfast at nine or ten with some cakes or rusks. An hour later he might have a biscuit with a glass of sherry. Dinner at two (or at three to four by 1780) might include chicken, venison, ham, a pudding, beans, some berries, and apricots. An elegant dinner would be much more lavish. There might be, for example, some cod, mutton, soup, chicken pie, pudding, roots, pigeons, veal, asparagus, sweetbreads, lobster, tarts, syllabubs, jelly, fruit, and a Madeira and port. Supper, at about 10 P.M., would consist of a variety of cold meats (Drummond and Wilbraham, *The Englishman's Food*, pp. 211–12). The wealthy Londoner would eat later: breakfast from ten to eleven, dinner at five or six, and supper very late in the evening. Again, the food would be varied and plentiful. A grand dinner served by the formidable Mrs. Delany included the following: beef-steaks, turkey, boiled neck of mutton, greens, soup, plum pudding, salmon, salad, onions, fillet of veal, peas, blancmange, Dutch cheese, cream, apple pie, mush-terrene, crab, cheesecakes, currants, gooseberries, orange butter, and, for dessert, strawberries and cream, raspberries and cream, and sweetmeats and jelly (Bayne-Powell, *Housekeeping in the Eighteenth Century,* p. 105).

Johnson preferred heavy, rich food. In 1782 he recorded in his diary the menu of a dinner at Streatham, the Thrales' Surrey estate: "I dined at Streatham on a roast leg of lamb with spinach chopped fine, the stuffing of flour with raisins, a sirloin of beef, and a turkey poult; and after the first course figs, grapes not very ripe owing to the bad season, with peaches —hard ones. I took my place . . . and dined moderately that I might not at the last fall into the sin of intemperance" (*Diaries, Prayers, and Annals,* pp. 337–38n). Johnson's concern that he not lapse into gluttony was appropriate in his times, as some of the menus already mentioned might indicate. Food was eaten in quantity by those who could afford it, and not only at great dinners. Of course, at a lord mayor's feast one would expect splendor (or at least plenty). Kielmansegge writes that at a lord mayor's feast in the early 1760s there were two large pieces of roast beef at the foreign minister's and another table, one weighing 227 pounds, the other 230 pounds (*Diary of a Journey to England,* p. 153). Individual diets of a striking nature were frequently reported. Dr. Cheyne, for example, ate one meal each day, consisting of a bottle of port, a quarter bottle of brandy, a tankard of ale, a trifle of broiled fowl or plate of fish, and a 1½-pound rump steak. It took him, on the average, about 1½ hours to finish. The "joints" of meat of which we read were often as large as thirty pounds, particularly a joint intended for a sizeable household.

The wealthy Englishman enjoyed certain exotic foods, such as peacock steaks or ortolans (imported in September, as a rule). Fowl were popular. (Those geese and turkeys which were driven to London had their feet tarred so that they could withstand the stones on the roads.) Salads consisted of such ingredients as lettuce, cucumbers, watercress, and mint. A dressing of oil, vinegar, and salt was generally used. There were over sixty varieties of puddings. The "portable soup" of which Boswell writes was stock reduced to a thick jelly, which was then dried in the sun.

As is apparent from the foods mentioned above, the eighteenth-century English gentleman loved meat. Saussure writes that "English people are large eaters; they prefer meat to bread, some people scarcely touching the latter" (*A Foreign View of England,* p. 220). Rochefoucauld estimated that "the consumption of meat is much greater in England than in any other country whatever; the whole nation eats it and the Englishman, generally speaking, is a flesh-eater" (*A Frenchman in England,* p. 204). Grosley also commented on the comparatively small quantities of bread eaten by Englishmen: "They, properly speaking, live chiefly upon animal food; and their beer furnishes them with a substantial and nourishing drink" (*A Tour to London,* 1:140). Foreign complaints about English food may have been justified, though the lack of perfection in his viands did not inhibit the hungry Englishman. Some visitors' comments are well known: for example, Zetzner's remark that an English dinner, lacking soup and dessert, is like eternity—it has no beginning and no end; or Voltaire's statement that the English have a hundred religions and only one sauce. The most common complaints in the eighteenth century are those which one hears now. As Rosamond Bayne-Powell writes, "It is curious that the three things with which the foreigner most often found fault, cooked vegetables, soup and coffee, are those which are most frequently criticized today. We do not seem to have learnt much in culinary art in the last two hundred years" (*Travellers in Eighteenth-Century England,* p. 16).

The rich and plentiful fare of the well-to-do was not without its unpleasant results. Addison's comments in 1711 were to hold true for years after:

> It is said of *Diogenes,* that meeting a young Man who was going to a Feast, he took him up in the Street and carried him home to his Friends, as one who was running into imminent

Danger, had not he prevented him. What would that Philosopher have said, had he been present at the Gluttony of a modern Meal? Would not he have thought the Master of a Family mad, and have begged his Servants to tie down his hands, had he seen him devour Fowl, Fish, and Flesh; swallow Oyl and Vinegar, Wines and Spices, throw down Sallads of twenty different Herbs, Sauces of an hundred Ingredients, Confections and Fruits of numberless Sweets and Flavours? What unnatural Motions and Counterferments must such a Medley of Intemperance produce in the Body? For my Part, when I behold a fashionable Table set out in all its Magnificence, I fancy that I see Gouts and Dropsies, Feavers and Lethargies, with other innumerable Distempers lying in Ambuscade among the Dishes. [*Spectator* 195]

Some of the problems resulted from the absence of refrigeration. A great deal of tainted meat was eaten, often served with honey or some strong sauce. London butcher shops, such as those in Butcher Row behind St. Clement's, often had unglazed windows. The meat hung on hooks, exposed to rain, dust, soot, and insects. It was difficult to keep animals alive through the winter. When they came off summer grass, all but the breeding stock were slaughtered and heavily salted. The breeding stock were put on short rations in hopes they would survive the winter. The fact that the meat was salted would account for the quantity of sweets and drink which would counter the effects of the salt.

One of the chief problems with vegetables was logistic. Kalm writes that "when farmers and others convey anything into the town to be sold, they seldom drive with an empty load home, but they mostly take a wagon full of this manure out with them from the places where it is collected together" (*Kalm's Account of His Visit to England,* p. 144). Fruits and vegetables were often fertilized with London night soil. They then made their trip to London in a wagon which had brought night soil on the previous trip. This would also be true of produce brought by barge, for the barge would convey manure from points such as

Butcher Row, looking towards Temple Bar. Note the head piked on Temple Bar and the unglazed windows on the butchers' shops.

the Whitefriars dung wharf. The vegetables also smelled of coal smoke. Grosley writes that the vegetables grown near London are "impregnated with the smoke of seacoal, which fills the atmosphere of that town," and they "have a very disagreeable taste, which they communicate to the meat wherewith they have been boiled" (*A Tour to London*, 1:72).

Problems with food were not, of course, confined to London. Seamen hit their ship's biscuit against something firm in an attempt to jolt loose the weevils and maggots in it. Sometimes they ate in the dark in at least semiblissful ignorance. Food preparation was often conducted in unsanitary circumstances. Kitchens were often dirty, kitchen workers sometimes black with filth. One of the poignant aspects of unattractive fruits and vegetables is the fact that they were also very expensive. Fruit, for example, was food for the rich. Some of this was sold from barrows and baskets. Matthew Bramble's complaint

The food of the poor.

to Dr. Lewis that some of this dusty fruit was cleaned with the spittle of the hawker is probably no exaggeration. Bramble also complains about the use of adulterants, a demonstrable problem.

A distinction must be drawn between adulteration and substitution. Moritz described English coffee as an "atrocious mess of brown water" (*Journeys of a German in England*, p. 35), and Archenholz wrote that "the most contemptible tradesman in all Germany drinks better coffee than [the English]" (*A Picture of England*, p. 203). The poor, however, could not afford coffee. They sometimes drank "horse-bean coffee," made from horse chestnuts. In this connection we should remember Johnson's comments to Mrs. Thrale, who was offended by

Billingsgate Fish Market.

by the smell of food which the poor could not often afford.

Adulteration might bring down prices in some cases, but the exchange was not always an equal one. In some cases the adulterants would be harmful. Milk would often be watered, and if we remember the quality of eighteenth-century water, that adulteration could be harmful. Small shopkeepers would sometimes put sand in sugar and sell horse or donkey as beef and mutton. White bread was prized, and it was thus adulterated with chalk, alum, bone-ash, white lead, lime, and sometimes wood ash. In addition to improving the color, some of these substances (alum, for example) improved the texture and increased the size of the loaf. Tea, which was very expensive as well as very popular, was adulterated with dust, small pieces of stick, and dried leaves, particularly sloe leaves and blackberry leaves. Sulphuric acid was sometimes sold as vinegar, and so were dilute solutions of oil of vitriol colored with burnt sugar or oak chips. Adulterated cheap wines and fake wines were commonplace. Color would be obtained from something like burnt sugar or blackberry juice; orange peel was used for flavoring, sugar for sweetness, and hops or oak chips for astringency. Rum was faked by coloring and flavoring cheap spirits with molasses. Beer was adulterated with water and with the Caculus India Berry. The neutral principle of this berry is picrotoxin, which can paralyze and cause convulsions, gastroenteritis, and excessive stimulation of the respiratory system.

The shopper always had to be wary of sharp practices. In some cases there would be help from official sources. For example, the Fishmongers' Company made attempts to curtail illegal activities. These practices included putting dead eels in with live ones and blowing up codfish to make them seem larger. In some cases dishonest merchants intercepted supply boats before they could make their way to Billingsgate. This would drive up prices, at which point those in London would sell.

There were many fish and shellfish from which to choose: salmon (the most expensive), carp, skate, trout, lobster, sole, and scallops, to name but a few. The sources of food and drink were many. One might purchase sustenance of various sorts at a coffeehouse, a tavern, an alehouse, or a cookshop. There were itinerant piemen and sellers operating out of stalls as well as bakers' shops and chandlers' shops.

The tavern meals on which Johnson and the members of the club dined were at first modest. At the Monday meetings they would have cold meat, cheese, wine, and punch. The menu changed when the meeting day changed: "In 1772, the day was changed to Friday, and the members dined together every other week during the sitting of Parliament. The meal was now a real 18-century repast: a soup, perhaps of green peas; then a stewed fish, accompanied by beans, bacon, salad, and a light meat course, such as veal or tripe; then roasted capons, with or without a beef dish as well, a veal dish, a venison pie, and sometimes stewed rabbits; and an ice or fruit for dessert" (Curtis and Liebert, *Esto Perpetua*, pp. 76–77). The rabbits might have been gelded. That was sometimes done in an effort to improve their flavor.

Johnson's demeanor at the table received comment from his contemporaries. Certain things should be kept in mind. In a city without centralized heating, for example, many would be overdressed at the table. As the company and the steamy, salted food increased in quantity Johnson would not have been the only one to perspire. Proximity to the fireplace would also be a factor. Anyone else suffering from emphysema (as Johnson did) would probably be breathing with some labor also. Moreover, eighteenth-century table manners were not models of decorous behavior. For example, finger bowls were sometimes used for rinsing out the mouth as well as washing the hands. One guide to table manners cautions diners against scratching, spitting, smelling the meat on their forks, blowing their noses, leaning their elbows on the table, and picking their teeth before the dishes are removed. They were also advised not to return from the necessary room readjusting their clothing. I am not denying that Johnson was a somewhat dramatic diner, but only suggesting that he may not have been alone in his behavior. It may well be that commentators seized upon his table manners as a *human* trait, something that linked him with others and reminded them that Johnson was a human being as well as an austere moralist and writer of consummate skill and seemingly limitless energy. We should remember too that Johnson was a demand eater. As he dined so did he fast. While he might eat with great relish, he did not have the ravenous maw of a Dr. Cheyne.

Given the city's somewhat primitive system of water supply one would think that much of the day would be given over to the carrying of water, for even the wealthy—whose water was piped into the home—received water only a few times a week or a few hours a day (it was then stored in cisterns, generally of lead and sometimes highly ornamented). In addition to the public pump one could collect rainwater or purchase water by the jug from "cobs." However, little time would be spent on securing water, for little water was used. None was drunk. It was so contaminated that many would let it settle for several days before using it. Immersion bathing was not considered to be a practice conducive to good health. Wooden bathtubs (used in bedrooms and filled from kettles) would be seen only in the homes of the wealthy; some had marble basins or fixed baths, but these were rare. Most people would use a basin and wash nothing but face and hands. A bath in the modern sense might happen annually or semiannually. Those who could afford it sometimes bathed in milk.

The homes of the poor differed markedly from those of the well-to-do. Although some were fortunate enough to have floors of flagstones, others (particularly the rural poor) had earthen floors, which were sometimes mixed with bullocks' blood and then tamped down. These were often strewn with herbs or rushes to hide the floor's appearance and its odor. For tableware the poor usually had sycamore platters or trenchers and maple cups and bowls. The lower middle classes might have platters and mugs of pewter. China and glass were not available at moderate prices.

Of the porcelains and chinas available to the wealthy, Wedgwood's were comparatively inexpensive. Flaxman the sculptor designed the decorative classical figures which adorned the Wedgwood works; many of the designs were copied from frescoes of Pompeii. The wealthy might also enjoy Chinese wallpaper, each piece of which was hand painted. Their floors were usually made of polished wood, which was sometimes inlaid, though stone and marble were also used. Staircases could also be made of marble, but more often walnut, cherry, mahogany, or pine was used. Doors were often mahogany with brass or ebony handles and locks of steel damasked with gold. Sash windows were insulated by shutters. Their lamps sometimes had crystal vases; their chimneys were sometimes made of Italian marble. One of the predictable fixtures in a wealthy home was the tea caddie. Caddies generally had two divisions, one for black tea, one for green. At times there was a center division for sugar. These would be locked, for both tea and sugar were expensive. The wealthy might also use pewter utensils or containers, but they would seek fine pewter, of copper, brass, and tin, rather than ordinary pewter of tin and lead.

The eighteenth century was a great age of style, an age of Palladian, Baroque, and some Gothic architecture. There were great architects like the Adams and great landscape architects like Brown. Not all could own an Adam house with its decorative details, but many purchased the furniture of Chippendale, Hepplewhite, and later Sheraton. Early furniture would often be of walnut veneer (on beech, or another cheaper wood), but solid oak was also used, especially in the provinces. Walnut was supplanted by mahogany, imported from the West Indies. The mahogany used for furniture was first polished with linseed oil, then coated with brickdust applied with a cork, and finally varnished. When the householder decorated his walls he first went to the color merchants for linseed oil and pigments; the painter then mixed the paint on the spot before applying it. The other appointments and appurtenances which one might find on a wealthy estate are too numerous to discuss here, but suffice to say that eighteenth-century imaginations were fertile. One might well find, for example, a clockwork cradle which, when fully wound, would rock for over forty minutes. Looking through the nursery window one might see a pseudo hermitage installed on the estate for color and atmosphere. There might even be an actual hermit, hired to grace the estate with his dour presence. Some had stuffed hermits on their grounds.

While single men might dine in taverns, families dined at home, and their kitchens were extensive, particularly rural kitchens which, in addition to sculleries, larders, and rooms for distilling, might also have adjoining dairies and bakehouses. A kitchen had a large open fireplace. Meats were roasted in front of the fire with the roasting jack being turned by the kitchen boy. In some cases dogs in cages were used to turn the spits. (Dogs were also sometimes used to power butter churns, as were horses.) Spits might also be turned by wound weights or by fans in the chimney which were turned by the heat and, in turn, moved the spit. Drippings were collected in a pan, and the meat was basted constantly. Some large chimneys were

Rowlandson: An inn kitchen with a dog turnspit.

used for smoking hams and bacon, with birch considered the best fuel to use. Cupboards with iron doors next to the fireplace were used to keep dishes hot, to mull wine, and to bake cakes and pies. Pots and pans were generally of iron. Hams were sometimes hung in canvas bags from the rafters of the kitchen. Bread was suspended in the air in a bread car (a kind of crate) to protect the bread from rodents. The homes of the wealthy were designed for the enjoyment of food but not for efficiency of preparation and service. Kitchens were often located remotely, and it would not be uncommon to have the silver washed in the dining room between courses and then reused.

A problem for both rich and poor was the need for artificial light. The "matches" which are sometimes referred to were wax tapers with bits of phosphorous. The match was sealed in a fragile tube. Immediate ignition occurred upon contact with air. Thus, while matches were portable and convenient, they were very dangerous. Most people resorted to the tinder box, which contained flint, steel, and pieces of charred linen rag. When sparks touched the tinder (the rag), it glowed. Before the glow died down, a match tipped with brimstone was inserted into the glowing linen. This was done very carefully so as not to inadvertently extinguish the linen. The rich used beeswax candles. Others made homemade candles of wicks dipped in melted fat or used rush lights, which consisted of rushes dipped in fat or grease and then placed in metal holders. Candle wicks were originally made of the pith of rushes. They were not consumed as the candle burned and thus required frequent trimming. Cotton wicks came later. When the lights were extinguished and the family retired, their beds might first be warmed with warming pans. The less wealthy might use hot bricks wrapped in flannel. Most families had mattresses of goose, duck, or fowl feathers, but the most demanding (and affluent) had beds of swan feathers.

The daily details of life were many, and those chores which are easily accomplished today would then be highly labor-intensive and time-consuming. Hence the wealthy had a large number of servants. For the single male like Johnson, the tavern would be of considerable importance, not just as a place to eat meals but also as a place to obtain cooked food to be eaten at home. For large joints in particular, the tavern would be Johnson's recourse. In the household of an intellectual with few or no servants many chores would simply not be done. The disarray which would result might easily occasion surprise, particularly for those who were long accustomed to the presence of servants. So too, the presence of broken furniture might surprise the wealthy, but for the often financially strapped Johnson, furniture which we would today take for granted (because of mass production) would be a luxury which he could not always afford and to which the vast majority of English men and women could never begin to aspire.

V. Travel and Transportation

The first impression of London which the tired traveler received was not necessarily a pleasant one. The smell of the air might be the first indication that London was within a few miles of the traveler's ship. If the visitor was coming by coach he might see the brick kilns which were located on the outskirts of the city. The kilns polluted the air and attracted an unsavory element searching for a place to sleep that might provide some warmth.

The foreign traveler who had just negotiated the Channel might feel some relief at the sight of English soil, for there were pirates in the Channel and their presence was a matter of concern for those making the crossing. Yet, once in England the traveler faced what some might consider pirates of a different order: the excise officers. It was not uncommon for a foreign vessel to be met by small craft whose occupants offered to transport the travelers' dutiable goods, thus bypassing the excise officials. The goods would be restored later, at a prearranged point, for a fee. Of course, those who accepted such services ran the risk of never seeing their goods again. Besides, allying oneself with smugglers was a dangerous undertaking.

Smuggling was a large-scale operation, particularly the smuggling of desired items such as tea, spirits, and lace. Pitt calculated that the 13 million pounds of tea consumed in 1784 probably included only 5.5 million pounds on which duty had been paid. The reduction of import duties finally reduced the smugglers' numbers, but for a time they were very active and potentially very dangerous. One event which caught the attention of the nation was the 1748 torture and murder of William Galley, a riding revenue officer, and Daniel Chater, an in-

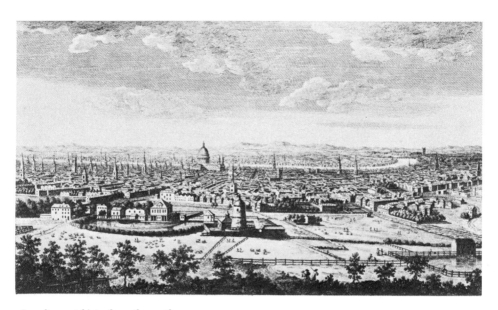

London outskirts, from the north.

former. A gang from West Sussex had arranged to receive a smuggled shipment of tea near the Hampshire border. The tea, valued at upwards of £500, was intercepted by a privateer, who took it to the Custom House at Poole. The gang broke open the Custom House, seized their tea, returned to Sussex, and celebrated their success. One spectator at their festive breakfast was Daniel Chater, a shoemaker, who had, on prior occasions, worked with one of the smugglers. Chater was later taken by the customs officers and was found, by the smugglers, with Galley. The smugglers assumed that Galley and Chater were there to ruin them and decided to kill them. They were tied to their horses. Galley "rode with his head under the belly [of his horse] . . . wounded, bruised, and hurt," with one of the smugglers "all the time squeezing his private parts." Then, after having "cut off his nose and privities, [and having] broke every joint in him," the smugglers decided he was dead. Galley was thrown into a hole and buried. Chater suffered in similar fashion and was hurled into a well. This was in February; their bodies were not discovered until the following autumn (Cal Winslow, "Sussex Smugglers," in Hay et al., *Albion's Fatal Tree*, pp. 136–37).

Corrupt excise and customs officials on the one hand and rapacious and inhuman smugglers on the other did not offer a pleasant choice. Grosley's experience was the best. He arrived on Sunday, when the customs officers were not working. His carriage was accordingly loaded with undutied kegs of brandy. Moritz's experience was more representative. Like many travelers, he left the Thames about ten miles from London to complete his passage by land: "This is the usual course taken by those who sail up the Thames, because of the astonishing mass of sea-borne traffic growing more and more congested as the city is approached. Often it takes several days for a ship to work a passage through these last few miles" (*Journeys of a German in England*, p. 23). He traveled by post chaise, which permitted three passengers to pay as one, at 1s. per mile. (As it turned out, his ship took three days to travel the ten miles to London.) He was then presented with the choice of bribing the excise officers or seeing his trunk taken to the Custom House. He chose bribery (6s. in all) and then hired a porter to carry his trunk to a waiting coach. The porter charged 2s.

Saussure's ship was boarded by customs officials who indicated that they would break the ship's wooden partitions as part of their search for illegal goods. After being bribed, they did not damage the ship but did search the passengers. Saussure was surprised that they even searched the women's petticoats (such a search being more intimate at a time when drawers were generally not worn), but when they did so, they found Flanders lace there.

The docks were not particularly safe, especially for the unwitting foreigner. Thus the German colony in London kept a watch there to protect their countrymen and help guide them through the world of the cutthroat and the custom house. This was a good idea. Moritz, for example, encountered a ship near Tower Hill which offered tours. Once the curious got aboard, they were forced to buy their way off or be pressed into naval service. The press gang particularly preyed on naive visitors

The Custom House.

from the country. The amount of crime on the docks, especially thievery, was incredible. Some stole cargo by having accomplices aboard ship drop the goods overboard. At low tide the goods would be retrieved. The retrievers were called "mudlarks."

The most striking aspect of the river, however, was the number of vessels upon it. Saussure estimated that "round about London there are at least 15,000 boats for the transport of persons, and numbers of others for that of merchandise" (*A Foreign View of England*, p. 94). "The Thames below the bridge is almost hidden by merchant vessels from every country" (ibid., p. 95). Between Windsor and Gravesend there were perhaps as many as 40,000 watermen. Kalm wrote that "it is impossible to express the untold multitude of ships and vessels which sail up and down the river daily, especially in the summer time, when ships in some of the narrower places can hardly avoid running into each other, and often at the same time cause each other great damage" (*Kalm's Account of His Visit to England*, p. 3). Kalm traveled in 1748. In 1784 Rochefou-

Travel and Transportation

Canaletto: Traffic on the Thames at Westminster Bridge.

cauld found much the same thing: "At London the river is so crowded with vessels that there is only just room for one or two to pass when they have business higher up the stream; in fact one can scarcely see the water, but only the forest of masts which floats above it" (*A Frenchman in England*, p. 10).

Saussure describes the vessels of the Thames watermen: "These boats are very attractive and cleanly kept, and are light in weight, painted generally in red or in green, and can hold six persons comfortably. On rainy days these boats are covered with coarse, strong tents, so that the rain cannot pass, and in summer, when the sun is burning hot, with an awning made of thin green or red woollen stuff" (*A Foreign View of England*, p. 169). From the bridge to Westminster the watermen of Saussure's time received 3d for a one-man boat, 6d. for a two-man boat. The price doubled if the bridge was passed. The oarsmen wore uniforms with embossed plates on their doublets containing the arms of their protectors, "for some of these boatmen belong to the King, others to the Prince of Wales and to different peers of the realm others again to the Lord Mayor or to the magistrates of London" (ibid., p. 170). The watermen solicited business with great energy and enthusiasm: "As soon as a person approaches the stairs these men run to meet him, calling out lustily, 'Oars, oars!' [a two-man boat] or 'Sculler, sculler!' [a one-man boat.] They continue this melodious music until the person who intends taking a boat points with his finger to the man he has chosen, and they at once unite in abusive language at the offending boatman" (ibid.). The job of a waterman was popular; those so employed were not pressed into naval service in time of war. To protect the traveler from gouging, maps were sold in London with indications of the fares between different stairs.

Prior to mid-century, the only bridge across the Thames was London Bridge. At Westminster, coaches crossed the river to Lambeth by horse ferry. A man and horse crossed for 2d., a horse and chaise for a shilling, a coach and six for 2s. 6d. Westminster Bridge was opened in 1750; its first stone had been laid in 1739. Built at a cost of £389,500, it was 1,223 feet long, 76 feet wide at its center, and had fourteen arches. The tides beneath it were as high as 22 feet. The arches echoed in such striking fashion that people played French horns beneath them; the more rustic blew hunting horns there. Westminster Bridge had a high parapet, some said to discourage suicide. The bridge was a fashionable place for walks and had alcoves which served as shelters for pedestrians. The alcoves were eventually removed because they became haunts for footpads. In its time Westminster Bridge was considered by many to be the finest in Europe. Unfortunately it was erected on the shifting river bed instead of on properly excavated footings. The bridge which Johnson and Boswell knew was taken down in 1859.

Westminster Bridge was wide enough to accommodate two paths for pedestrians and a thirty-foot roadway for carriages, but the need remained for more bridges. Johnson saw the construction of the bridge at Blackfriars, which was opened to wheeled traffic in 1769. He had, in fact, written proposals on the manner of its construction on behalf of a friend. *The bridge*, however, has always been London Bridge.

Blackfriars Bridge.

When the Romans came they found two rounded hills on the Thames, the eastern hill, the site of Leadenhall Market, and the western hill, the site of St. Paul's. They built their basilica on top of the eastern hill and bridged the Thames in such a way that the bridge would run to the foot of the eastern hill. The London Bridge which Kielmansegge found in the 1760s was very near the site of its Roman predecessor: "The Thames being 915 feet wide at this part, this is the length of the bridge, and the width is 31 feet for carriage traffic, with 7 feet on each side for foot-passengers" (*Diary of a Journey to England*, p. 187). Until mid-century one of the striking features of London Bridge was the series of structures erected upon it. There were shops as well as private dwellings. These were taken down in the late 1750s. If one looks at pictures of the bridge two important things are apparent. First, the height of the bridge does not permit access to large, high-masted vessels. Thus, the bridge was the terminus for much traffic. Second, the piers beneath the bridge both hindered and endangered traffic. It was necessary to "shoot the bridge," and under certain condi-

Below London Bridge. Note the current under the bridge.

tions this could be very hazardous. Hence the increased fare on the part of the Thames watermen for taking their passengers beyond the bridge. Drownings beneath the bridge were common. One of the key features of life on the bridge was the frequency with which one would hear the cries and screams of those drowning beneath the bridge's homes.

The vitality and the sheer press of numbers and vessels at this point on the Thames is difficult to imagine now, but we must remember that the Thames was wider in the eighteenth century than it is today. In its waters were trout, shad, lampreys, barbels, roach, dace, eels, flounder, salmon, porpoises, and an occasional sturgeon. In the mid-seventeenth century a fifty-eight-foot whale was killed between Deptford and Greenwich.

Travel on the Thames, particularly in the less crowded waters above London Bridge, was efficient and colorful. Readers of Boswell know that it was common for travelers to hurl insults at one another in a spirit of competition. Travel by water, like travel by horseback, has an air of reality and risk about it. Johnson, with his fellows, traveled in this fashion, and we should keep it in mind as we build our own image of the ethos of the period.

Travel by coach, enjoyed and praised by some, was a different affair altogether. It was conducted in a variety of ways, few of which would appeal to the twentieth century. The first thing which must be said about eighteenth-century land travel is that conditions varied greatly from road to road, season to season, and day to day. In general, travel improved markedly as the century progressed. The turning point was approximately the middle of the century, for the Jacobite rising of 1745 had raised logistics problems which emphasized the necessity of improved roads. Yet with all its problems, English travel was usually easier than that on the Continent. Kielmansegge wrote that "no country is so well arranged for comfort and rapid travelling as this" (*Diary of a Journey to England*, p. 18). He had come to England for the coronation of George III, landed at Harwich and dined at Colchester. The fifty-mile trip to Ingatestone took ten and a half hours, but a speed of less than five miles per hour was not at all out of the ordinary. In most cases a brisk walk provided quicker travel than an eighteenth-century coach. John Metcalf, the road builder, once refused a seat in the London to York coach. He preferred walking, he said, and in point of fact, the coach was so delayed by floods and bad road conditions that Metcalf arrived, on foot, before the coach did.

Travel by road was not for the uninformed, for only main roads had signposts. One could very easily become lost. Hardy Englishmen rode horses. There was the danger of highwaymen, of course, but this mode of travel enjoyed certain advantages. For example, the muck, mire, and ruts of the road could be avoided. In some cases, one could travel in a straight line and avoid the bends of the roads. Enclosure would make horseback travel more and more difficult, but it was common throughout the period. Foot travel was not. Those with means almost never walked. In the few cases when they did, they would certainly be armed. Anyone else found walking would be considered, *a priori*, either a footpad or a pauper. Moritz

Travel near the city: Oxford Street.

walked the London–Oxford road. He saw very few pedestrians, many coaches, and many on horseback, "which is here the usual mode of travel" (*Journeys of a German in England*, p. 120). Moritz found innkeepers to be inhospitable, partly perhaps because he was a foreigner, but chiefly because they feared anyone on foot was either a beggar or a rogue. They told him in sullen fashion that they had no rooms. They refused to let him sleep on a bench, at bed prices, when he suggested such an arrangement.

Given public attitudes and the state of the roads, Johnson's walks to and from Birmingham would have been perceived as very odd, apart from any considerations of melancholia. The nature of the terrain there would also call the practice into question. Campbell wrote that "the country between Bermingham & Litchfield [is] the worst I have yet seen in England, it is bare naked & of shallow soil, not so hilly as the county Cavan but almost as bad—near Litchfield it improves" (*Campbell's Diary of a Visit to England*, p. 92).

Moritz walked for different reasons than Johnson, but he was no luckier when he traveled by coach. Coaches were designed to carry four passengers in comfort inside. However, they usually took six inside and also allowed people to ride on top, a hazardous as well as uncomfortable prospect, particularly in an early-eighteenth-century springless coach. No more than six were supposed to ride on the top but sometimes as many as twelve to fifteen rode there. Thus, in the case of low limbs, projecting buildings, or bad road conditions, the trip would be interrupted by the climbing down and climbing back up of the passengers on top of the coach. Delays would be tedious and frequent. The ruts in the road were sometimes very deep (Arthur Young saw ruts four feet deep in 1770), and passengers would either climb down until these had been negotiated or, in some cases, be bounced off of the coach. Moritz, taking the coach from Leicester to London, was forced to ride outside. He was bounced into the air and, fortunately, landed on the coach. After this mishap he chose to ride in the luggage basket, or "rumble tumble" (against the advice of his fellow passengers), where he was very badly bruised and shaken. He then managed to get back on top of the coach. Covered with dust he sat there as it began to rain.

The reason for people to cling desperately to the top of a lurching coach, exposed to the elements, was quite simple. Travel was expensive, particularly travel which afforded any degree of comfort. Scott paid £4 10s. for a trip from Edinburgh to London, but with meals, tips, and stops the trip finally cost him nearly £50. The degree of "comfort," of course, was purely comparative. In 1762, Boswell traveled from Edinburgh by post chaise, a polite mode of travel in which there would be but one other passenger. Before reaching Berwick one of the wheels of the chaise became inoperable. The driver proposed that they ride to Berwick on horseback. Boswell chose a three-hour delay and a new chaise. Between Stamford and Stilton an unruly horse caused the chaise to overturn.

Hogarth: Coach with riders atop and "rumble tumble."

Boswell hurt his arm, Stewart (the fellow passenger) his head. Traveling at night, and in fear of robbers, they both rode with loaded pistols in their hands. Boswell's statement, "When we came upon Highgate hill and had a view of London, I was all life and joy" (*London Journal*, p. 43) is, to say the least, understandable.

Very few would be able to afford travel by post chaise. Still, as Rosamond Bayne-Powell writes, "We may conclude that a journey was then about the most expensive thing a man could undertake" (*Travellers in Eighteenth-Century England*, p. 10). A rough rule of thumb for travel would be 2½d. per mile in summer and 3d. per mile in winter, but this would vary based on the type of conveyance taken. The post chaise, which became common at mid-century, generally held two passengers. There was no coachman; instead, the horses were driven by a "postboy" (a man, actually) who rode on one of them. The fee would include a tip of 3d. a mile, 1s. 6d. per mile for posting, and 6d. for the ostler when the horses were changed. This was very expensive travel.

The stagecoach, or diligence, was far cheaper: 2d.–3d. per mile with tips at the end of the journey for the guard and coachman. The coaches were heavy and, in the early century, had no springs. They were drawn by two to four horses and would travel at four miles per hour or less. Earlier in the century they were drawn by three horses with a postboy sitting on one of them. In cold weather straw was placed on the floor of the coach for the passengers to put their feet into. Coachmen were romantic figures, particularly in the eyes of the young. They sipped brandy and water and sometimes filed off their front teeth, so that they could better handle the whip cords which they carried in their mouths.

The stage wagon was more economical, but far less romantic. It was actually an immense cart with benches. It was covered by a canvas or leather hood and drawn, at a walking pace, by eight horses with the wagoner walking. The stage wagon made two miles per hour or less, usually traveling in the daytime. It did not change horses and charged 1d.–1½d. per mile. Stage wagon travel was somewhat safer than coach travel, for highwaymen assumed that the wagon passengers would not be worth robbing. Many women—among them Johnson's mother —traveled in this fashion.

Once in London the traveler could use a hackney coach (London's were numbered from 1 to 1,000) or a sedan chair. A hackney coach with two horses charged 1s. for one and a half miles; a sedan chair with two chairmen, 1s. per mile. Those with means could travel by private coach. Reynolds' coach, for example, was particularly fine. It featured both painted panels and carved and gilded wheels.

Travel times and schedules are not reliable, for times were estimated with shillings in mind rather than the realities of the road. For example, in the 1730s a coach advertised that it went from London to Exeter in three days. Everyone knew that the trip required six days. As a rule of thumb, a coach might make fifty to sixty miles a day on improved roads in good condition.

At mid-century one could travel from Birmingham to London in two summer days. Bath was a two-day trip from London, Manchester a trip of four and a half days, Edinburgh a journey of ten days. Frequency varied. In 1740, for example, there were three coaches to Bath from London leaving three times a week, and five coaches weekly to Harwich. Coaches to York, Newcastle, and Edinburgh left the Black Swan in Holborn three times a week in summer, but only twice a week in the winter. The coaches often started very early—for example, at 2 or 4 A.M.

The Oxford machine traveled to and from London daily. It took six passengers for 10s. each. It did not stop for breakfast, and it allowed each inside passenger twenty pounds of luggage (above that, there was a charge of 1d. per lb.). Outside passengers paid half fare (the usual pattern). The fact that the coach did not stop for breakfast was no deterrent. Travel sickness was very common. Many went to bed without supper upon their arrival at their destination for they were upset, shaken, and ill from the ride. Children in laps were often charged the same half fares as outside passengers.

All times were affected by road conditions, which were particularly bad in the winter months. Kalm noted that straw and other litter were thrown on wet roads to improve traction. Later it was shoveled into heaps, left to rot and ferment, and then used as manure. Prior to the granting of trusts for the maintenance of roads (and the charging of tolls) surveyors of roads were appointed by the magistrates of the parishes. It was the surveyor's responsibility to see that local residents with property over a certain value provided six days of labor each year for road maintenance. What actually happened, when it happened, was that people were hired and money collected from the rate-payers. The turnpikes were an improvement but also a nuisance. Rochefoucauld, for example, found four toll-houses in the twenty-seven miles between Bury and Cambridge. Three of them charged 6d. for the carriage; the fourth charged 9d.

The problems of the traveler were either relieved or increased once he arrived at an inn. Accommodations were rank-oriented, in that they were geared to the type of conveyance in which the traveler arrived. For example, the most elegant place at which to stay the night was the posting house. Posting houses generally entertained those who had arrived in their own private coach. Some of the posting houses would accept passengers from the mail coach, but none of them would consider taking in passengers from the common stagecoach. These people would have to go to inns. The inns would generally not accept pedestrians or wagon passengers. In some cases they might take them into the kitchen and allow them to purchase the remains of the evening meal. The wagon travelers and those on foot would have to go to hedge inns, where they might pay 9d. or a shilling for a bed and supper.

At most inns travelers were presented with a pair of used slippers to wear during their stay. The state of such slippers was probably, to put it mildly, disreputable. Even at very good inns it would be common to share rooms, and in many cases, beds, with strangers. Traveling through the countryside Moritz surprised people with his going on foot, but impressed them with his London hat, which he had purchased for a guinea. He records the type of food which he found at the inns: "I lunched here on a piece of cold meat and salad. Either these or eggs and salad were my usual midday and evening meals in the inns where I stayed. I seldom got anything warm. They gave me the ingredients for the salad but I had always to mix them myself, as is the custom here" (*Journeys of a German in England*, p. 175).

The mail coach was a very important communications link in the eighteenth century. Londoners early in the century enjoyed a penny post for local mail. Any parcel weighing a pound or less went for the same price as a simple letter. Mail went to different destinations on different days. For example, early in the century letters went on Tuesdays to Germany, Holland, Sweden, Denmark, North Britain, Ireland, and Wales; on Wednesday to Kent and the Downs; on Thursday to Spain, Italy, and all parts of England and North Britain. Letters returned on specified days—for example, from all parts of England and North Britain on Mondays, Wednesdays, and Fridays; from Kent and the Downs from Monday through

Saturday. Postage fees were based on weight and distance. A single sheet traveling eighty miles would be 2d.; a double sheet traveling more than 80 miles, 6d. A double sheet to Dublin cost 1s.; a double sheet to the West Indies, 2s. 6d. Members of Parliament sold pre-franked materials to nonmembers. In 1763, for example, approximately seven million franked letters were posted.

The other vital link in the communications network of the eighteenth century was the newspaper. The newspaper and other periodical publications are beyond the scope of this study, but a few general statements should be made. The century saw the birth and demise of hundreds and hundreds of papers, both in London and in the provinces. There were far more papers, with far smaller circulations, than the modern reader is accustomed to; papers were read and reread; many were shared. The Englishman was hungry for news, and the London papers provided it. Provincial papers frequently reprinted material from London papers, and many Londoners folded their papers, addressed them to friends in the countryside, and posted them. A foreign traveler in the streets of London would not find the specialized magazines that are found today, but he would find far more newspapers—arguing political points of view—usually with circulations of 3,000 copies or less. The papers depended more on sales than on advertising for their income. One of the most striking differences between eighteenth-century journalism and that of today is the fact that virtually every major eighteenth-century writer—Defoe, Addison, Steele, Pope, Swift, Fielding, Johnson, Boswell, Burke, Goldsmith, Smart, Smollett—wrote at some time in his career for periodicals, and much of this material transcends the levels generally associated with hackwork. While many major cities today produce but a few papers, most of which are of little literary or intellectual value, the papers of eighteenth-century England continue to be the subject of serious scholarly investigation.

VI. Health
and Hygiene

We have already discussed a number of the aspects of eighteenth-century life which either impaired health or, at least, posed a threat to health. In addition to London's fog and damp there was smoke from industry and from private dwellings. Sanitation was poor and filth was everywhere, including the domestic kitchen and upon the preparers of food. Many did not enjoy a balanced diet, and what food could be afforded was often adulterated. Air and light were denied to many because of the governmental tax on windows. We do not hear the coughing of London's eighteenth-century residents when we look at pictures of the period, but we often see cripples and various victims of disease or ignorance there.

As Lawrence Stone and others have noted, the eighteenth-century physician could diagnose but few diseases with certainty, among them plague and smallpox. At his disposal were very few effective remedies. Quinine could be used for fever and ipecacuanha for dysentery. Smallpox could be prevented through inoculation, which had been introduced, from Constantinople, by Lady Mary Wortley Montague. Unfortunately, the practice of inoculation did not spread quickly. Children, who were very susceptible to the disease, were often not inoculated, and in some cases imprecise methods of inoculation resulted in the contraction of true smallpox. The process itself was quite unpalatable, with threads being passed through pustules of the diseased and the substances then introduced into the healthy through the use of incisions which were sometimes too deep. To encourage the spread of inoculation, some held inoculation parties, but the disease continued to kill about one in thirteen of every generation until the widespread practice of vaccination in the nineteenth century. In the eighteenth century the incidence of smallpox was such that masters often required guarantees that their servants had already had the disease. Some servants advertised this fact in the newspapers as they looked for employment. Smallpox was one of the few diseases for which a servant would be sent to the hospital. The prevalence of smallpox, and of smallpox scars on the faces of people, should be a part of the modern mental image of the eighteenth century. It is one of those eighteenth-century paradoxes that Lady Mary Wortley Montague was not only an important promulgator of medical advance but also one of those individuals whose personal filthiness was proverbial.

The eighteenth century offers a very different medical picture from that to which modern readers are accustomed. Diseases which are now either conquered or very rare were regular killers in the eighteenth century. For example, in 1774 in London, 49 people died from cancer, 4,242 from consumption, 5,457 from convulsions, 743 from dropsy, 2,607 from miscellaneous fevers, 121 from measles, 2,479 from smallpox, and 780 from problems arising with their teeth. The list is not exhaustive. Thrush, which is comparatively rare now, and which results from filth and malnutrition, claimed 88. Cases of rickets were common, of course, and many children suffered from bacterial infections and (as Queeney Thrale did) from worms. The prevalence of worms was one of the few justifications for the violent purges and emetics to which one would have then been subjected. Johnson, whose body was wracked by numerous diseases and afflictions, was not as abnormal then as one might think.

In addition to medical ignorance, many were subjected to hazardous circumstances. For example, all those who might work with metal—plumbers, glaziers, pewterers, letter-founders, and others—were doubtless exposed to such substances as lead and mercury for extended periods of time. And it was not only the craftsmen and tradesmen whose bodies would come into contact with dangerous substances. The cosmetics used by eighteenth-century women (and by some men) often contained mercury and lead. Women painted their faces, necks, chests, and arms, sometimes starting as early as age fourteen. In so doing they ruined their skin, suffered allergic reactions, sometimes lost their hair, and developed gastric disturbances. Some died. Black coloring around the eyes was obtained through the use of lamp black or the residue of burned ivory shavings. Lip salves were common, and linen-lined leather was strapped over the forehead at night to remove furrowed brows. Night vizards purportedly did the same for wrinkly cheeks. High brows were popular. Plucking was common. One item that was recommended for high brows was a forehead bandage which had been dipped in vinegar in which cat excrement had been steeped. This was still popular in the nineteenth century and, though unappealing, is not surprising, for animal and rodent dung were common ingredients in many eighteenth-century medicines.

Readers of *Tristram Shandy* are familiar with Dr. Slop's "somewhat bushy and unctuous" wig. It is probable that the powdering of wigs originated in a desire to absorb grease, but the powdering later became cosmetic. Wigs were sometimes made of human hair, sometimes of horsehair, sheep's wool, goat's hair, and hair from the tails of heifers. Wigs were powdered to counter the association of grey and white with the aging process and also to make the eyes appear brighter. Grey powder was common until 1720 or so, and was succeeded by white powder. In some cases hair was darkened by combing it with a leaden comb. If the wig was to be powdered, rice or wheat meal might well be used, but first the wig would be greased so that the powder would adhere to it. A woman's coiffure might last two weeks. Women of fashion slept propped up in bed and had their hair retouched daily and repowdered two or three times daily. The greased and powdered wig served as a haven for vermin; it was thus necessary to "open the head" once a week or so and apply ointment to counteract the effects of the vermin. Slender, hooked rods were used to scratch the head. These were sometimes of ivory, silver, or gold and could have jeweled handles. Given the high proportion of the population wearing wigs, men's haircuts were usually near-shavings. Sometimes "borders" were used—half wigs which blended into the person's natural hair. White, blonde, and jet black wigs were particularly expensive; brown and light chestnut wigs were more common. In the 1770s and 1780s women's hairdos were particularly striking. Many were very high and built on wire foundations. Blown-glass models (for example, of windmills or butterflies) were perched on the hair—a hazardous practice at a time when candles burned in chandeliers. In some rare cases such hair could afford protection. Here is an extract from Hampden's *Journal,* based on contemporary news accounts of London in the mid-1770s: "A fellow who sat on the sixth row of the Upper Gallery of Covent Garden Theatre, threw a keg (which he had brought full of liquor into the house) over the gallery front. It fell upon a lady's head, who sat in that part of the pit which was railed into the boxes, but the lady's hair being dressed in high *ton,* the artificial mountain luckily prevented the mischief that otherwise might have been occasioned" (p. 253).

Clothes were endangered by exposure to dirty bodies as well as to foreign objects and theatre missiles. Physical cleanliness was not an eighteenth-century ideal. Underwear was generally worn as protection for the outer clothing and not as protection for the body. Men's drawers were tied at the knees and closed by a string; Englishwomen generally did not wear drawers until the very end of the eighteenth century. The women who could afford it perfumed their smocks. The wealthy gentleman wore a coat of silk, satin, or velvet, a waistcoat, breeches, silk stockings, a white linen shirt, leather shoes with decorative buckles and wooden heels, and sometimes a sword. For travel he wore a long cloth cloak. He often carried his hat because he was already wearing a wig. Women wore dresses of silk, damask, brocade, and later, muslins and cottons. They wore corsets, plain linen shifts, and gartered stockings, particularly green ones, though white became fashionable after the 1730s. The women's shoes were high-heeled and clumsy; the heel was too far under the instep for comfortable walking. Around the house, slippers were a welcome substitute. Outside, cloaks and hoods (especially scarlet and, later, black ones) were worn. Later, straw hats with ribbons over lace caps were popular. In the eighteenth century English men and women kept abreast of French styles through the use of "fashion babies," dressed dolls which were regularly sent from Paris to London. In a period when the bizarre was often commonplace, one of the more striking fashions was the post-Revolution, 1790s technique for imitating the aristocrats who had gone to the guillotine. Englishwomen wore thin crimson ribbons around their necks and had their hair tousled, in a style termed *la victime coiffeur*.

False bosoms were achieved through the use of wirework, false buttocks through the wearing of cork attachments. Men sometimes wore artificial calves—an indication of virility—while some women wore pads or cushions to simulate pregnancy. Children—both male and female—wore frocks. Boys were breeched at about six or seven in the seventeenth century, at age three or four in the eighteenth. Infants were swaddled well into the eighteenth century. For about four months the child could move neither its head nor its limbs. It was then enabled to move its arms but not its legs. Parents feared that a child's movement could result in broken or misshapen extremities. There were other results instead. The heartbeat was slowed. This reduced crying and induced sleep. Moreover the child could be left unattended. The physical and psychological effects on the child of immobility and long-term contact with waste materials were doubtless harmful. The importance of avoiding sensory or motor deprivation in the early months of life is now commonly recognized. Young women were often encased in tight corsets, iron collars, and backboards to improve their appearance and posture, sometimes with disastrous results. There are accounts of girls being so tightly laced that their ribs grew into internal organs and caused death.

The lack of concern for hygiene plus poor facilities and techniques for cleansing resulted in a malodorous social setting. It has been suggested that fans were used to allay the effects of bad breath as well as for the purpose of flirtation. This was not an affliction of the poor alone, who could not afford dental care. Walpole's breath, for example, was notoriously fetid. Breath sweeteners such as bramble leaves, cinnamon, cloves, honey, burnt alum, and orange peel were sold to those who could afford them. Body odor was countered with perfume, cologne, and many fragrant waters (not with soap), and rooms were perfumed with pastilles burned in incense pots.

Teeth were a prime cause of infection, disease, and death. Treatment was primitive. For example, some had nerves severed in their ears to relieve the pain of toothache. False teeth were generally of bone or ivory, wired in place with a baseplate of wood. Tinctures, powders, and tooth sticks were used to whiten teeth. Teeth were scoured with abrasive sticks made of such substances as powdered coral or pumice. Cavities were drilled by hand and then filled (very carefully) with molten lead, tin, or gold. The process was not pleasant.

Day-to-day life—with which Johnson was so concerned—was made painful for all by the continual presence of vermin. Andrew Cooke, a bug-destroyer, advertised that in twenty years of work he had rid 16,000 beds of insects. If he was not successful upon the first attempt, he would return to complete the job without any additional charge. In respectable households bedsteads were disassembled and washed each year. The floors were scoured, and rue was sprinkled about. The later use of iron for bedsteads had a direct impact on the problem of verminous beds. So too, washable cotton clothing was finally substituted for wool. Because the wool could not be washed, lice and other parasitic insects were able to thrive there. China came to be used instead of wooden vessels, and brick and stone were substituted for wood as a construction material, thus rendering the rat's task of gnawing an entranceway far more difficult. The growing dominance of the Norwegian, or brown, rat over the English black rat was also to result in improved health, for while the black rat lived in homes, the brown generally stayed in sewers, granaries, or docks and carried fewer infections to man. The battle would always be an uphill one, for the streets were filled with substances such as excrement and butchers' offal which would attract vermin.

The health of the poor was materially improved through the so-called Dispensary Movement. The first such dispensary was founded in 1769 for the relief of the infant poor. The General

Dispensary, better known than its Red Lion Square predecessor, was founded the following year. The dispensaries delivered health care as well as medicines. Without such aid medical help was beyond the means of the poor; they would not summon a physician until the patient was on his deathbed.

Even so, what medical care was available was primitive by modern standards. Johnson, who had been touched by Queen Anne in an attempt to have his scrofula cured, did so on the advice of a physician. Johnson always defended the medical profession, but it is not unfair to say that the state of medical science lagged far behind the scientific advances in physics and chemistry in the Renaissance and eighteenth century. One could, in fact, practice medicine without taking an examination, unless one contemplated military or naval service or

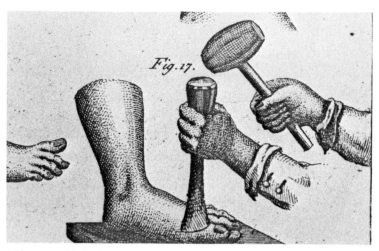

(Above and left) *Amputations. From Dr. James's* Medicinal Dictionary.

resided in Oxford, Cambridge, or a locale where a barber's guild or company was in control, such as London, Newcastle, York, and Bristol. It has been said that the medical profession was less concerned with health care and patients than with the pecking order within the profession. That this was true in some cases is clear; that it was not universally true is also clear. At the top of the list of practitioners stood the physician, cultured and educated but with no knowledge of surgical procedures. Then came the surgeon, a skilled but sometimes rough technician. The barber-surgeon had no hospital appointment, and the apothecary, who sold nostrums and sometimes looked at patients before consulting with a physician, ranked with the barber-surgeon above the midwife. Beneath the midwife were the unlicensed practitioners and, finally, the quacks. Quacks would sometimes hire individuals to simulate fierce diseases which the quack would cure in near-miraculous fashion.

Early in the century the Royal College of Physicians would admit only students from Oxford, Cambridge, or Trinity College, Dublin, to full membership. Those who studied at European schools or at Edinburgh could be made licentiates of the College. The surgeons—originally members of the Company of Barbers—separated and founded their own company in 1745. The apothecaries, originally members of the Grocers' Company, served as the medical men for the majority of the population.

The overall problem besetting eighteenth-century medicine has been described by Richard Shryock:

> Viewed calmly and in retrospect, one can see that this period was one of protracted struggle between the old and the new. Certain aspects of medieval rationalism lingered in those sciences in which it was most difficult to establish modern methods. The same conflict had occurred in the physical sciences during the seventeenth century; but there it had been relatively short and incisive because of the relatively prompt triumphs of Newtonian mathematics. Rationalism in medicine was partly replaced, but in part simply disguised by the new philosophy. [*The New Development of Modern Medicine,* p. 37]

The eighteenth-century medical student still had difficulty obtaining cadavers. Opposition to dissection survived until after the mid-nineteenth century. Physiological experimentation was, for most, unthinkable. Thus, some operated on themselves for experimental purposes. John Hunter, for example, inoculated himself simultaneously with gonorrhea and syphilis. Medical specialization was heartily discouraged, and a clear professional line was drawn between general medicine and surgery.

Surgery was conducted without anesthesia, of course, and generally as a last recourse after much pain and anguish. The patient was usually given a glass of brandy and restrained by three or four assistants. Because of the lack of anesthesia, surgeons operated quickly. In some cases Cheselden could remove a stone from the bladder in thirty seconds or less. His death rate was about 17 percent, primarily through hemorrhage, infection, or shock. He treated the poor free of charge, but others were assessed a fee of £500. A good surgeon could

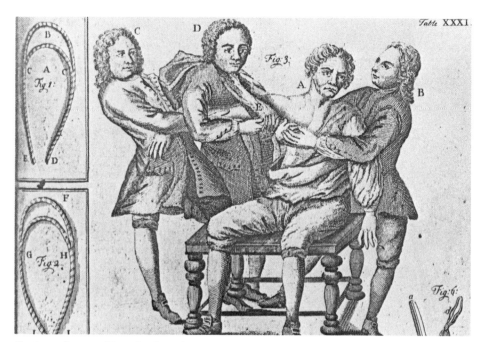

Setting a fracture. From Dr. James's Medicinal Dictionary.

amputate a leg in four minutes or less, sometimes in only two. Caesarian sections were rarely attempted; they would be far beyond the skill of the average practitioner. One of the problems attending lack of skill and cleanliness was that comparatively minor fractures or wounds would often end in amputation of the affected limb. Among the more common treatments for physical ailments were bleeding, or phlebotomy, clysters (enemas), blistering, and cupping. These were routine treatments, and references to them recur in the diaries of the period.

Some medicines (Peruvian bark, squills) were of positive medical benefit. Others bordered on the fiendish, in practice if not in intention. One remedy for the stone, a common eighteenth-century affliction, consisted of egg shells, soap, and snails. Walpole, who suffered from the stone, took both soap and lime water as medicine; it has been estimated that he

EXPECTORANTIA. Medicines which promote Expectoration, or a Difcharge of any thing which is offenfive to the Lungs, and Afpera Arteria.

Among the feveral Species of Evacuants, none are, perhaps of more Importance than thofe which eliminate the vifcid Lymph fecreted from the arterial Blood, and remaining in the Glands, or rather the glandulous Coats and Emunctories. But in no Part of the Body is there a larger Secretion of mucous Lymph than in the internal Ducts of the Afpera Arteria, and the Bronchia of the Lungs, which are internally lin'd with a glandular Coat: Hence very often a ferous, pituitous, vifcid, and, fometimes, a purulent Matter, is, in Coughing, expectorated, and efpecially in Diforders immediately affecting the Lungs, whether of the acute or chronical Kind. The Medicines which promote this Evacuation from the Cavity of the Thorax are call'd *Expectorants*; of which the moft confiderable in the Vegetable Kingdom are, the Roots of Elecampané, Arum, Florentine Orris, and Liquorice; the Herbs Paul's-betony, Chervil, Scabious, Moufe-ear, Germander, Hyffop, and the Tarragon; the Flowers of Violets, Mallows, red Poppies, and Saffron; the Seeds of Anife, and Fennel; the Bark of Saffafras; and, among refinous Gums, Benjamin, and Gum Ammoniac; among Fruits, Raifins, Figs, Jujubes, and Pine-kernels; Honey, Liquorice-juice, and Oil of fweet

From Dr. James's Medicinal Dictionary.

consumed 180 pounds of soap and 1,200 gallons of lime water. Some remedies were simply zany. One bit of advice for those with jaundice was as follows: hard boil an egg in the patient's urine; prick the shell of the egg with a pin and bury it in an anthill. As the egg wasted away, so should the disease. Alternatively, one could treat jaundice by ingesting nine live lice each morning. Persistent bleeding, it was suggested, could be stopped by soaking the testicles in a bath of very strong vinegar.

Snail tea and horse-dung possets were not uncommon. For

coughs and bronchitis some swallowed a broth made of two puppies and a stewed owl. Cockroach tea was taken for kidney disease, and toothaches were treated by taking powder made from the eyes of pikes. For apoplexy, pigeon's blood was used, for epilepsy tortoise blood. A bolus of spiders was sometimes taken against fever. For whooping cough and ague some consumed fried mice. The delicate and the consumptive drank asses' milk, which was generally more expensive than cows' milk. Rotten apples were made into a poultice for sore eyes; watercress was rubbed on the head for baldness. One nostrum for smallpox specified the use of thirty to forty dried, powdered toads.

Given the high incidence of gaol fever and other diseases in the city's prisons, it was feared that defendants would infect the judge, jury, and attorneys. Thus, herbs were spread in courtrooms to form a barrier between the accused and the rest of the people there. Despite that "precaution" there were instances of diseases being communicated to others in the room. From a medical point of view, trials would sometimes be hazardous enterprises.

One of the principal disinfectants was vinegar. We have already seen it prescribed to counter disease. Vinegar was used to cleanse money, particularly in time of plague. Doctors carried canes with round balls on top filled with vinegar. When John Howard, a sheriff of Bedford, was conducting his study of later-eighteenth-century prison conditions, he changed his clothes after visiting a facility and smelled vinegar for further protection.

Perhaps the most popular of eighteenth-century medicines was the fever powder concocted by Johnson's friend Dr. Robert James. George Washington took it, as did George III. Goldsmith is reputed to have died of it. The powder was composed of antimony and phosphate of lime. Johnson, wisely, had doubts about the efficacy of James's compound medicines. He was clearly in the minority, however, for they sold widely. One of Johnson's saltier surviving comments concerns James. James was an old friend but also a lecher who once offended Johnson by picking him up in a coach in which

MASTUPRATIO, or MANUSTUPRATIO. Manual Stupration, a Vice not decent to name, but productive of the most deplorable and generally incurable Diforders. Thus we have given a remarkable Hiftory, under the Article AMAUROSIS, of a Series of Diftempers caufed by this abominable and unmanly Practice. And, under the Article GONORRHOEA, to this we have attributed the moft obftinate Gleets. Befides thefe, incureable Impotence, Lownefs of Spirits, hypochondriacal Diforders, and almoft all Sorts of chronical Diftempers, are excited by it. And it is worthy of Remark, that People accuftomed to fuch Filthinefs, are not fo eafily cured of chronical Diftempers, as others who are Strangers to it. For, as *Celfus*, fpeaking about Venereal Intercourfes, prudently remarks, *Cavendum, ne in fecunda valetudine adverfæ præfidia confumantur.* That is, "We fhould " take care, during Health, not to lavifh away that Strength of " Conftitution which fhould fupport us in Sicknefs."

From Dr. James's Medicinal Dictionary.

he was riding with a prostitute: "James apologized by saying that he always took a swelling in his stones if he abstained a month &c— Damn the rascal says Johnson, he is past sixty the swelling wd. have gone no farther" (*Dr. Campbell's Diary of a Visit to England*, p. 68).

Murphy claimed, on Garrick's authority, that in enumerating the greatest human pleasures, Johnson ranked sex above drinking. The remark has always come as something of a surprise to scholars because it comes from Johnson. As a remark issuing from the eighteenth century, however, it would probably elicit little surprise, for the period is often associated with rakes and sparks, double entendres, low décolletage, and women of the town.

In point of fact, however, there may have been less sexual activity than one might expect, particularly in the lower classes. For one thing there was little education in this area. There were sometimes waxwork exhibitions of anatomy and reproduction for educational purposes. There were also a number

*Sir Francis Dashwood, a notorious eighteenth-century rake, at his "devotions."
Dashwood and his companions repaired to Medmenham Abbey for their sexual
activities.*

of physical conditions which would inhibit sexual activity. Bodies were unwashed and frequently verminous. Breath would be fetid from both stomach disorders and tooth decay. Eczema, scabs, and running sores were common, and there was always the likelihood of contracting venereal disease or the fear of unwanted pregnancy. Leukorrhea, inflammation, and vaginal ulcers would result in painful intercourse. Both poor diet and exhaustion have an adverse effect on sexual drive, and the eighteenth-century worker would often add to these a history of chronic disease. Marriage might be a matter of convenience rather than affection, and it would often come later in life, after patterns of auto-eroticism had been established. Generalizations are meaningless when we are speaking of individuals, but it is quite likely that in the population as a whole there was less sexual activity then than now.

This is not to suggest that celibacy was common, only that sexual activities probably occurred on a smaller scale. Among the advertisements in eighteenth-century periodicals, ads for cosmetics and books took second and third place to ads for venereal disease cures. One person in the mid-1770s was refused a patent for a venereal disease nostrum on the grounds that if it were successful it might serve to encourage vice. Venereal disease found its way into all levels of society. Boswell is no exception here. Henry Thrale paid 50 guineas for treatment for a venereal complaint; Mrs. Siddons contracted venereal disease from her husband. For the upper classes there were also homosexual clubs in London. The public response to homosexuality and to homosexuals placed in the pillory was often very severe.

There were abortionists—both chemical and surgical—in London, but they were probably patronized by few. Birth control devices were largely unavailable. Prostitutes had condoms, but more for prophylactic than contraceptive purposes. Made of sheep intestine and secured with ribbons, they were available in both London and Paris, but in London at only one or two outlets. Widespread use of such devices did not occur until the vulcanization of rubber in the 1840s.

When pregnancy did occur, delivery was not always easy.

Hogarth: A prostitute. Note flagellation rods on the floor and condom on the table.

Many midwives had no formal training, and many of them had other employment. For example, a midwife might be a fishmonger or hawker of vegetables and assist deliveries only periodically. Part of the midwife's oath included a provision that she seek to ascertain the identity of the father of the child. Illegitimacy brought with it expenses to be borne by the public.

Thus, it was quite common for the midwife and other local women to cross-examine the woman in labor and refuse her help until she identified the father. In some cases mothers assigned the responsibility for paternity to rich men in the neighborhood who were able to pay (and who were then forced to pay for maintenance of the child).

Hospital care, on the scale to which modern readers are accustomed, was not always available. Hospitals were supported by subscribers, and admission to hospital services was contingent upon receipt of a letter of recommendation from a subscriber. Typhus was rampant in hospitals because of infestation, and many poor were excluded from hospitals because of the frequent requirement that the patient present a deposit or security to indemnify the hospital for burial charges.

Grosley was very impressed with the cleanliness he found at Chelsea Hospital: "The refectories of our richest Benedictine monks are hog-sties in comparison of that of this hospital" (*A Tour to London,* 2:47). The cleanliness was, of course, relative: "The invalids are allowed two shirts a week, and every year new bed cloaths. The great love of cleanliness, natural to the English, has made the place of matron one of the most important and honourable employs belonging to this hospital" (ibid., p. 47). Grosley's impression should not be generalized. Most hospitals were plagued by vermin and overcrowding. Physicians sometimes wore short coats so that they would not brush against the walls and beds and pick up lice. Three to four adult patients per bed—lying head to foot to head—would not be uncommon, and as many as eight infants might share a single bed. Hospital workers often carried sponges soaked in vinegar, which they would press to their nostrils for protection.

In the eighteenth century death came quickly and frequently. Infant mortality was such that siblings were sometimes given the same name, on the assumption that at least one would not survive for long. (Foundlings were often given the name of the parish in which they were found; at Johnson's church there were many young Clements.) In the early eighteenth century as many as 74 percent of London children died under the age of two. In 1764 49 percent died by the age of two, and 60 percent by the age of five. The infant was subject to smallpox, fever, worms, poisoning from pewter dishes and from lead nipple shields, rickets, excessive swaddling, and a general lack of fresh air. The situation improved after mid-century. Midwives, particularly male midwives, became more skilled. Efficient forceps were developed—far less dangerous than the hooked instruments which injured mother and new-born child alike. Inoculations against smallpox were more common, and washable cotton materials resulted in better hygiene. Yet the situation was still very difficult, and wealth did not insure protection. Seven of Mrs. Thrale's twelve children did not live past the age of nine. The strong, however, might live long lives. Susanna lived to 88, Cecilia to 80, and Hester Maria (Queeney), 92.

Because of financial conditions marriage sometimes came comparatively late. An upper-class woman might marry in her early twenties; a wealthy heir might marry in his mid- to late twenties, while his younger brothers would often not marry until their mid-thirties. In the lower classes both men and women married in their mid- to late twenties. These marriages were often short in duration, not because of divorce—which required an act of Parliament—but because of early death. The average marriage among the poor lasted about twenty years or less. A marriage in the squierarchy might last a bit longer. The duration of Johnson's marriage, short by modern standards, was quite ordinary by eighteenth-century standards. The remarriage rate was high; perhaps 25 percent of all marriages were second marriages for one or both of the parties. Menopause came comparatively early, and the reproductive period was comparatively short. The rich had larger families than the poor, for the rich man could marry a young woman, and the rich often did not benefit from the contraceptive effects of lactation because they often used wet nurses. They did not suffer the exhaustion and malnutrition of their poor countrymen and the reduced libido and fecundity which accompany those conditions.

We think of the eighteenth century as an age of many wars, and so it was, but, as has often been pointed out, the ravages of disease were more deadly than the results of muskets and grape. In the Seven Years' War, for example, for every man dying in battle there were eighty-eight who died of disease. For many soldiers, life alternated between fear of the lash and fear of the pox. Corporal punishment was very severe. One soldier boasted that in fourteen years he had endured 26,000 lashes, 4,000 of them in a single year. If a soldier deserted he was hanged. He was disciplined with the whip, while his female companion was disciplined with the whirligig, a chair in which one was strapped and spun until sickness and vomiting were induced.

For the soldier death could bring relief. For the Londoner death was a quite different affair. Funerals were elaborate. The family issued invitations, usually decorated with skulls, coffins, and skeletons. Mourners were presented with rings, sometimes of precious metal or fashioned from the hair of the deceased. Pallbearers wore black gloves and black silk hat-bands. Women known as "wakers" sat up with the dead; for this they were generally given a pair of gloves. In the seventeenth century the poor children from Christ's Hospital were used as mutes at funerals (one of their other duties being the drawing of tickets at public lotteries). Eminent people commonly lay in state after their deaths. The dead were buried in wool shrouds with pillows in their coffins.

Undertakers were very competitive. Tipsters were paid to inform them of sickness and impending death, with fees set in proportion to the gravity of the illness. The undertaker's fees were complicated by steps necessary to circumvent the grave robber. Grosley writes: "I have been told that the precautions necessary to be taken in order to secure dead bodies from the craving anatomists, greatly increase the expence, by making it necessary to dig graves of an enormous depth: in a word, a bill which I was shewn of the expences for burying in a church-yard a child of one of the lower sort of people, aged three years, amounted to two guineas" (*A Tour to London*, 1:307). Giants were the particular prey of the anatomist. John Hunter bought the skeleton of Charles Byrne, an eight-foot, four-inch Irishman, for a sum of £500. A "corpse watcher" had been hired to inform him of Byrne's death. In order to foil the suppliers of cadavers—known then as "resurrection men"— one giant arranged for a twelve-foot grave carved out of rock and encased in iron bars and brickwork. The resurrectionists were, however, assiduous workers. In March of 1776 the remains of twenty dead bodies were found in a shed in Tottenham Court Road. The bodies were kept there by those trading with the surgeons. The report noted that in the Borough one dealer made no attempt to hide the nature of his profession and went by the name "the Resurrectionist." In the eighteenth century, birth, death, burial, and "re-birth" could be eventful occasions.

VII. The Law and
Its Enforcement

The eighteenth century is associated, quite properly, with pickpockets, footpads, and scapegraces, with highwaymen, smugglers, and thief-takers, constables, forgers, and hanging judges. The lives of criminals like Jack Sheppard and Jonathan Wild were written and rewritten, and lurid, often pornographic details of criminal acts were available to readers of the *Newgate Calendar*. Some criminals were loathed by the public; others were romanticized. Together the assortment of lawless men and women added both color and very real danger to the life of the eighteenth-century Londoner.

Modern observers are struck by the number of capital crimes in the eighteenth century, many of which seem trivial in their significance. Part of this surprise results from our forgetting that an item of very little value today (a handkerchief, for example) was of far greater value then, and the punishment for its theft much more severe. The other factor which must be kept in mind, one to which we will return later, is the fact that there was virtually nothing in the way of an organized police force to enforce the law. Harsh penalties and dramatic public executions were to serve as deterrents. Lacking police, the eighteenth century substituted intimidation and severe laws. In practice the laws were not always enforced to the letter. Many who were condemned were not executed, and juries were often merciful. For example, if a thief were to be sentenced to death for stealing forty shillings worth of merchandise, the jury might assess the goods which were stolen at less than that amount.

This is not to suggest that there were no executions. Tyburn, Newgate, Charing Cross, Tower Hill, and sometimes the scenes of the original crimes were locales for public hangings.

Beheading the rebel lords, Great Tower Hill, 1746.

The march to Tyburn occurred every six weeks. On average there were probably ten to fifteen executions at a time. What is sometimes forgotten is that children could be executed as well as adults. Only children under the age of seven were safe, although children between the ages of seven and fourteen were generally not executed. Some fourteen-year-olds were executed for their participation in the Gordon Riots, and there are records of fourteen- and fifteen-year-olds being executed for thievery. In attempting to elicit support for a bill for a London police force in the 1780s, the solicitor-general pointed out that nine of every ten criminals hanged in London was under the age of twenty-one.

Not all were hanged. Execution by the axe was considered a privilege in comparison with the rope. Peers condemned to be hanged could be executed with a silken rope as a final privilege. Eighteenth-century hanging resulted in death by slow strangulation. Generally there was no sudden drop and no severing of the spine. The condemned would hang for a long period of time. Thirty minutes would probably be a minimum; many remained there much longer. Survival was not unheard

Rowlandson: An execution outside Newgate.

of; some apparently came to life again on the dissection table, to the astonishment of the surgeons present. Thus, resuscitation schemes like Boswell's plan to save John Reid, the sheep-stealer he defended, were not as fanciful as one might think. Archenholz writes of the plan to resuscitate Dodd, the forger, and Johnson told of a plot to bribe the Newgate turnkeys to release Dodd, a plot which included the fabrication of a wax model of Dodd which was to be placed in the prison in his stead.

In order to hasten the strangulation process, friends and relatives of the executed would often hang on his feet and legs. Some criminals jumped in the air as the cart moved, drawing their knees to their chests, so that they would fall with a jerk. The battle with death was often succeeded by a battle with emissaries from the College of Surgeons. The surgeons had

Rowlandson: The pillory at Charing Cross.

the rights to the bodies of the executed, but friends and relatives could, if they wished, purchase the corpse. In some cases, deals were not clearly struck, and a squabble ensued. It would not be uncommon to see a scuffle between the surgeons' messengers and the members of the family over the body of the executed.

As we have already indicated, a sentence to the pillory could be a sentence to death, depending on the demeanor and mood of the crowd. The rich could hire guards to keep the crowd at a safe distance and the poor could sometimes depend upon their wits. Hampden notes the case of a pilloried deer-stealer on whom the crowd took pity. He sang for them, from the pillory, to their delight. In other cases the crowd was merciless. In one instance, two homosexuals were put in the pillory ("mollies," to the crowd). One was badly maimed. The other was short, and his feet would not reach the ground. He hung in the pillory, bleeding from nose, eyes, and ears as his face discolored. The crowd continued to pelt him.

The crowd administered quick justice. While executions were intended to discourage crime, they often occasioned it, for such public gatherings always attracted pickpockets and other petty criminals. The crowd, when it discovered a pickpocket at work, might whip and duck him mercilessly. On Tower Hill, for example, where one would find mountebanks as well as gibbets, a thief might be found and carried to Tower-ditch, where his ducking might be sufficiently severe to result in death. At the very least the crowd would subject those who did not meet with its approval to verbal abuse. Foreigners were singled out for special attention in this regard.

The corpse of a notorious criminal might be hung in irons after his execution, sometimes at the locale where the original crime was committed. In some cases the body was disembowelled, the head shaved, and the entire corpse dipped in tar before it was hung. Saussure describes a process he observed: "They are first hung on the common gibbet, their bodies are then covered with tallow and fat substances, over this is placed a tarred shirt fastened down with iron bands, and the bodies are hung with chains to the gibbet, which is erected on the spot, or as near as possible to the place, where the crime was committed, and there it hangs till it falls to dust" (*A Foreign View of England,* p. 126).

Highwaymen were sometimes hung in chains along the roads they once patrolled. Lawless seamen of various kinds—pirates, mutineers, deserters—were hung in irons along the Thames. Pirates were hung at Execution Dock, Wapping, at low tide and stayed there until three tides had flowed over them. Military executions, by firing squad, occurred in Hyde Park (also a very popular place for duels). Soldiers were flogged—savagely, in some cases—in St. James's Park.

Many went to their deaths with quiet resolve, some with élan. Boswell discusses the trial of Simon, Lord Lovat, beheaded for his connection with the Jacobite rising of 1745: "When asked if he had any questions to put to Sir Everard Fawkener, who was one of the strongest witnesses against him, he answered, 'I only wish him joy of his young wife.' And after sentence of death, in the horrible terms in cases of treason, was pronounced upon him, and he was retiring from the bar, he said, 'Fare you well, my Lords, we shall not all meet again in one place.' He behaved with perfect composure at his execution, and called out *'Dulce et decorum est pro patriâ mori'* " (Life, 1:181n). Not all would go to their deaths quoting Horace's *Odes*, but in the eighteenth century such things were possible. In other circumstances silence was essential. Some suspected criminals were subjected to the press, or *peine forte et dure* (hence the prison "press yard"). A criminal who refused to plead his cause could not have his possessions forfeited to the crown. Thus, some kept silence under torture to protect their families. Saussure (who also saw the execution of Jonathan Wild) describes the press:

> [It is] made use of when an accused person refuses to plead or contest the authority of the tribunal over him. In these cases he is stretched on the ground, his feet and hands are tied to stakes, and on his stomach is placed a plank with weights, more weights being added every four hours. The accused remains without food in this position until he consents to plead his cause and to recognise the validity of the tribunal. Cases have been known of criminals preferring to die in this fashion, after two or three days of atrocious suffering, rather than by the hands of the executioner, and this in order not to leave a mark of infamy on their families, and to save their possessions from going to the Crown according to the law. It is, however, very rarely that the King makes use of this privilege, and almost always gives up these possessions in favour of the families of the criminals. [*A Foreign View of England*, pp. 119–20]

In some cases the authorities used a preliminary torture in which the thumb was compressed with whipcord. In 1721 a woman named Mary Andrews tolerated this until three separate cords had been broken in the process. Only with the fourth cord did she agree to plead. This practice was not abolished until 1772. Even after that women could still be burned to

Peine forte et dure.

death, a practice which survived until 1790, but many women were strangled before the fire was started.

While some were willing to pay £5 for travel to the American colonies, others were transported there for crimes, a fate which some considered more severe than the death penalty. Most were sent to Virginia and Maryland to work for tobacco planters. In the early 1770s approximately a thousand per year were transported, 25 percent of whom were women. Many suffered from gaol fever and mortified toes during the transportation process. In the late 1780s criminals were again transported, but this time to Australia. In the interim, the war with the colonies interrupted the process, and the solution to crowded prisons was the imprisoning of felons in hulks on the Thames, where they did such work as dredging and ditch construction. Their lives were not easy. They were chained together with some two to three feet between them. They slept on bare boards. There were no clergymen and generally no physicians, though the hulk was regularly smoked with sulphur and washed with vinegar. Many were ill with scurvy, venereal disease, and other afflictions. The food allowance per six convicts every twenty-four hours was one-half of a bullock's head, some water, four pounds of biscuits, and some broth thickened with bread and oatmeal.

Perhaps the most common crime in eighteenth-century England was thievery. Moritz divided English rogues into three classes. Pickpockets, in his judgment, were highly skilled and, among thieves, genteel. Highwaymen carried pistols, although these were often unloaded; Moritz thought that many were kindly men. Footpads, on the other hand, were vile and low. Lacking the highwayman's horse, a footpad was likely to murder as well as steal since he had no means of escape. There were also house-breakers (burglars) and many confidence men and swindlers. Saussure felt that "no cleverer pickpockets exist than in this country" (*A Foreign View of England*, p. 92). Every crowd presented a potential threat, as Saussure learned by sad experience: "Quite lately a valuable snuff-box was stolen from me. I had placed it in the pocket of my carefully-buttoned waistcoat; my coat was buttoned likewise, and I was holding both my hands over the pockets of my coat. It is true the theft occurred in a very narrow, crowded street, or more properly called passage, leading into a park. These rascals are so impudent, they steal even under the gibbet" (ibid., p. 130). At least one pickpocket had a set of folded artificial arms which gave those sitting near her a false sense of security while she picked their pockets.

Some who fell afoul of the law might end in Bridewells—prisons for vagrants and prostitutes which took their name from Bridewell Prison, itself used for such inmates. There were prisons for debtors, such as the Marshalsea and the Fleet, as well as a number of prisons for other criminals. None were pleasant; in many the conditions were appalling. In studying later-eighteenth-century prisons John Howard found gross overcrowding. Many prisoners were confined to cramped cells for fourteen to sixteen hours a day. Sometimes the floors of the cells and dungeons were covered by an inch or two of water. The air was rank: "My reader will judge of its malignity, when I assure him, that my cloaths were in my first journeys so offensive, that in a post-chaise I could not bear the windows drawn up: and was therefore often obliged to travel on horseback. The leaves of my memorandum-book were often so tainted, that I could not use it till after spreading it an hour or two before the fire: and even my antidote, a vial of vinegar, has after using it in a few prisons, become intolerably disagreeable" (*The State of the Prisons,* p. 13). In many gaols and in most Bridewells, Howard reported, there was no allowance of straw for prisoners' bedding. When it was available, it was not changed for months, so that what straw prisoners had was often nearly worn to dust. Prisoners lay on rags instead or, in some cases, upon the cell floor. Howard claimed that Bridewell was the only prison in London which provided straw or other bedding.

In some prisons all were confined together—men, women, young, old, debtors, felons—and few prisons separated men from women in the daytime. In some gaols lunatics were confined and kept in cells with other prisoners. Gaol fever was rife. Howard noted that prisoners of war were often treated far better than gaoled Englishmen, the reason being that the government was sometimes reimbursed for maintaining the prisoners at the conclusion of the war. Needless to say, most

Mary Young, the pickpocket with false arms.

who were incarcerated were verminous, much more so than their friends outside.

The prison diet was, to say the least, spare. Debtors had no legal claim to food. In about half the prisons they received the normal allowance of bread, but if such an allowance was not forthcoming, they depended on the charity of friends, relatives, and passersby. At best they would receive little more than 2 pennyworth of bread a day (about 15–17 ounces). Some prisoners were served "water soup" (bread boiled in water), but there was little fresh water itself. In some Bridewells and in many county gaols there was no food allowance at all. Distribution and sale of food was the right of the keeper. In general, prisoners were famished. They left gaol barely able to move and were incapable of serious labor for weeks.

Children were gaoled (for example, for theft), and familes of debtors sometimes accompanied debtors to prison. The number of debtors in prison often exceeded the number of felons. When Saussure wrote, in the 1720s, he estimated the number of imprisoned debtors in London to be between eighty and one hundred thousand. Howard gives the following figures for the spring of 1776 (see accompanying table). To that set of statistics one should probably add two dependents per prisoner, the number of distressed thus exceeding 12,000 (*The State of the Prisons*, pp. 35–37).

	Debtors	Felons	Petty offenders	Total
Greater London	1,274	228	194	1,696
Other 39 counties	752	617	459	1,828
Welsh counties	67	27		94
City/town gaols	344	122		466
	2,437	994	653	4,084

Prisoners were often branded, though a well-placed bribe could convince the brander to use a cold iron. Exploitation through bribery was, in fact, a virtual way of life. Newly arrived prisoners were forced to pay garnish ("footing," or in some London jails "chummage") to other prisoners or forfeit their clothing. The money was sometimes used for an evening of drunkenness; hence, the gaoler (who generally had a financial share in the sale of liquor) overlooked the practice. Debtors were often forced to pay more garnish than felons. Some gaolers would put prisoners who did not pay bribes in irons. The Newgate garnish was 2s. 6d.; a gaoler might exact 2s.–5s. a week for the removal of irons. (Since many gaolers received no salary, their only means of support were the prisoners.) If a prisoner was permitted to live outside the prison proper, but within its liberties or "rules," the gaoler was first paid and surety given that the prisoner would not jump bail. Having paid the warden, the prisoner then found preposterously high rents for the rooms available within the liberties. The boundaries of the Fleet liberties were as follows: from Ludgate Hill, north, to the Old Bailey; from the Old Bailey to Fleet Lane; down Fleet Lane to the Ditch or Market and by the ditchside to Ludgate Hill. Though the liberties were not expansive, the area was packed with chandlers' shops, brandy shops, gambling cellars, and taverns where quick marriages were performed.

The prisoner continually found himself entangled by the law and the manner of its administration. Depending on where the quarter sessions and assizes were held, a prisoner in the provinces might have to walk ten or fifteen miles (in irons) to his trial. In some counties "gaol delivery" came but once a year. It was possible to spend twelve months in a disease-ridden facility only to be declared not guilty at the end of the incarceration. In Hull at one time the assize was held every seven years. The only good side of this situation was that key witnesses might die in the interim, and the prisoners, guilty or not, would be acquitted. Some acquitted prisoners, however, were imprisoned all over again because they were unable to pay the fees demanded by the clerks of assize and clerks of the peace. Prior to the mid-1770s an acquitted person might also be returned to gaol to pay fees to the gaoler or sheriff.

The situation was not always desperate. There were some kindly gaolers like Abel Dagge, keeper of Bristol Newgate Gaol and the gaoler of Richard Savage (singled out for high praise by John Howard as well as by Johnson). In general, the decentralization of the prison system resulted in quite varied situations from prison to prison, even within a single city. The following are examples of conditions taken from Howard:

NEWGATE

Gaoler, Richard Akerman
      Salary, £200
      Fees, Debtors 8/10; Felons 18/10; Misdemeanors or
      Fines 14/10; Transports 14/10
      License, for Beer and Wine
Prisoners
      Allowance to Debtors and Felons: a penny loaf/day
      Garnish, Debtors 5/6; Felons 2/6

Numbers,	Debtors	Felons
March 1, 1776	38	129
Dec. 26, 1776	33	152

Chaplain, Rev. Mr. Villette
      Duty, Sunday twice; every day Prayers; once a
         month Sacrament
      Salary, £35
Surgeon, Mr. Olney
      Salary, £50, for all Prisoners

Some perquisites came with salaries; the Chamber of London provided beef for the debtors and sometimes for the felons. Bedding at 1s. 3d. per week with two in a bed was available. Debtors paid discharge fees of 8s. 10d., felons 18s. 10d.

THE FLEET

Warden, John Eyles
      Deputy Warden and Clerk of the Papers,
         Daniel Hopkins
      Salary —
      Fees, £1: 6: 8 on entrance, 2/ to the turnkey
      License, for Beer and Wine to John Cartwright, who
         holds of the Warden on lease the Tap

Newgate Prison, as rebuilt in 1780.

Prisoners
     Allowance, none
     Garnish, 2/

Number,	in the house	in the rules
April 26, 1774	171	71
April 2, 1776	241	78

Chaplain, Rev. Mr. Horner
     Duty, Sunday twice; Wednesday Prayers
     Salary —
Surgeon, none

Howard did not see a table of fees which would, for example, account for the warden's lack of salary. He counted 243 prisoners on April 6, 1776. Their wives, children, and paramours numbered 475.

TOWER HAMLETS GAOL

In Well-Close Square
At a public house, kept by a Swede who also served as gaoler.
The prison rooms were once used for French prisoners. The
prison is out of repair and not secure. The keeper receives no
salary. Fees are 9/1. There is no table but there is an allowance of a penny a day. No straw. In May 1776: 1 prisoner
there.

TOTHILL-FIELDS BRIDEWELL

Keeper, George Smith
       Salary, £50, with £20 to the widow of the former
          keeper
       Fees, 5/2
       License, for Beer and Wine
Prisoners
       Allowance, a penny loaf and a penny a day each
       Garnish, 1/4
       Number, April 22, 1774 — 38
               March 4, 1775 — 109
               Jan. 8, 1777   — 110
Chaplain, none
Surgeon, Mr. Glover
       Salary, £20
Discharge fee — 4/2 and 1/ for the turnkey.

THE MARSHALSEA

Deputy Marshal, Thomas Marson
       Substitute, Thomas Phillips
       Salary —
       Fees, 10/10
       License, for Beer and Wine. The Tap let.
Prisoners
       Allowance, none
       Garnish, 3/6. It is called Ward-dues for Coals &c.
       Number, March 16, 1774 — 167
               May 15, 1776   — 234

Chaplain, Rev. Mr. Cockane
      Duty, Sunday
      Salary, 1/ from each Prisoner on discharge.
Surgeons, Messrs. Stapleton and Walshman
      Salary, 1/ from each Prisoner on discharge.

Pirates were committed to the Marshalsea along with debtors. The prisoners not liking the tapster's beer, they had beer brought in from a nearby public house (600 pots on one Sunday in 1775). The discharge fee was 1s. 8d., the keeper's fee, 4s. 8d.; the turnkey's fee, 1s. 6d.

LITCHFIELD CITY GAOL

No yard, no water, no straw. Keeper's salary £2. Fees 13/4. No table. Allowance 1/6 a week. Nov. 20, 1773: 2 prisoners; Jan. 8, 1776: 1 prisoner.

The administration of justice in eighteenth-century England was not unlike that of medieval times. Unpaid justices of the peace were chosen from the gentry by the lord lieutenant of the county. They were responsible for levying the county rate, maintaining bridges and roads, licensing taverns, administering poor laws, and supervising Bridewells, prisons, and workhouses. They were aided by constables, similarly unpaid citizens who took yearly terms of office. Magistrates receiving regular incomes were not instituted until the early 1790s. In a system such as this there was, needless to say, considerable corruption. Those who served without salary often found their money elsewhere, particularly in the form of bribes. "Trading magistrates" were common. One man, for example, received £36 a year for a job which he had purchased for £40—the salary was only a fraction of the money he could expect to receive. The conscientious often had other pressing duties and paid others to take turns as constable. The city or town watchman was called a "Charlie," for his office dated from Charles II's time (as "Bobbies" were instituted during the time of Sir Robert Peel). Grosley describes them accurately: "London has neither troops, patroll, nor any sort of regular watch; and it is guarded during the night only by old men chosen from the dregs of the people; who have no other arms but a lanthorn and a pole; who patrole the streets, crying the hour every time the clock strikes; who proclaim good or bad weather in the morning, who come to awake those who have any journey to perform; and whom it is customary with young rakes to beat and use ill, when they come reeling from the taverns where they have spent the night" (*A Tour to London*, 1:48–49). Charlies were paid through the levying of the parish watch rate. They generally met for duty at the parish "round house," which, as often as not, was actually octagonal. In London in the course of a considerable disturbance the magistrate could also call a squad of guards from the Tower. The magistrate not only adjudicated but also superintended raids and arrests. The job was not without hazard; assaults on thieves' cellars or disorderly houses could bring fierce retaliation.

Despite the relative informality of the system of law enforcement and its attendant problems there was stern opposition to an organized police force. When Shelburne suggested in the House of Lords that the Gordon Riots had brought the time for such a force, he was viewed as an apologist for the despotism associated with France. One exception was the establishment of the Bow Street runners, administered by Henry Fielding's brother John. Armed with cutlasses and their officers also with pistols, they patrolled at night and during meetings and gatherings of large numbers of people. The Bow Street runners were more a special branch than a sizeable force, but Fielding deserves credit for his work with them as well as for his many humanitarian enterprises.

Perhaps the major point to keep in mind when considering the eighteenth-century system of justice is the system's relative lack of structure and formality. The order in society had to come from individual self-discipline and maintenance of order without the constant presence of authority. Lawrence Stone describes the situation in this fashion: "It was precisely because of [the] underlying unity of the elites, and of the largely unquestioning habits of deference by those below, re-emphasized daily in action and in prayer, reinforced by the solemn ritual of

Sir John Fielding.

the death sentence and execution of lower-class criminals against property, that the state apparatus could remain so relatively weak in eighteenth-century England without a total collapse of social order" (*The Family, Sex, and Marriage*, p. 223). This judgment is accurate so long as one does not assume that the Englishman in the streets was docile and slavishly deferential. This system of justice should be kept in mind when we consider Johnson's comments on "subordination." Those remarks take on quite different meaning in a society without police, a society in which far greater responsibility falls on the individual than they would in an authoritarian, rigorously structured society.

That the law was not always applied evenly—particularly when considerations of rank interposed—cannot be denied. Aristocratic street toughs might inflict considerable pain and yet escape with a fine of a few shillings. These bullies, sometimes called "Mohocks," terrorized the watch and the people in the streets. Not all were aristocrats. They sometimes slit noses. Some were called "Hawkubites" because they trapped people between them, playing the hawk and buzzard. One of the

Mohocks' favorite forms of abuse was termed "tipping the lion": they squeezed the nose against the face while gouging the eyes with two fingers.

In *Spectator* 324 Steele discusses the "Dancing-Masters" who "teach their Scholars to cut Capers by running Swords thro' their Legs" and the "Tumblers," "whose Office it is to set Women upon their Heads, and commit certain Indecencies, or rather Barbarities, on the Limbs which they expose." In *Spectator* 332 Steele receives information on another variety of Mohock, the "Sweater":

> It is, it seems, the Custom for Half a Dozen, or more, of these well-disposed Savages, as soon as they have inclosed the Person upon whom they design the Favour of a Sweat, to whip out their Swords, and holding them parallel to the Horizon, they describe a sort of Magick Circle round him with the Points. As soon as this Piece of Conjuration is perform'd, and the Patient without Doubt already beginning to wax warm, to forward the Operation, that Member of the Circle towards whom he is so rude as to turn his Back first, runs his Sword directly into that Part of the Patient wherein School-boys are punished; and, as it is very natural to imagine, this will soon make him tack about to some other Point, every Gentleman does himself the same Justice as often as he receives the Affront.

Some rolled women down the street in barrels, while others knocked over sentry boxes. Gay writes of some "wits" who urinated on the sentry's box in order to embarrass women passersby, and of the "nickers" who broke windows by throwing coins (usually half-pences) through them. In the 1770s the town was plagued for a time by a group of acid throwers who set out to ruin expensive clothing, particularly the silk gowns of women.

Some took horses into shops (especially china shops), stole dogs from the blind, and tossed beggars in blankets. In some cases waiters were thrown out of windows and the outraged proprietor told to "put him on the reckoning." The Irish were fond of "houghing," or hamstringing, their opponents—that is, cutting the tendon and laming the victim for life.

The English system of justice in the eighteenth century should be seen within the larger context of the period's approach to social services, an approach that was both decentralized and constantly subject to abuse. The system presupposed a conscientious, responsible citizenry but brought with it instead lethargy and corruption. It is possible that this aspect of daily life stimulated and encouraged the century's interest in the concept of human nature, for the social system required the best, but often showed the worst, of which humans are capable. We have already discussed the apprentice system and the manner in which, in Dorothy George's judgment, it was virtually doomed at the outset. Roads were originally to be repaired by local residents, who were to give six days a year of unpaid labor. Streets in London were to be lit by residents. Parishes were responsible for law and order, care of children and of the aged, treatment of the sick, and help for the disabled and unemployed. In some cases there were private benefactors and efficient systems. In many cases there were not. From 1722 to 1782 parishes were permitted to build workhouses. Those who sought charity from the parishes with workhouses were lodged there, and with the consent of the majority of the parishioners, the poor could be put to work. They were hired out, often in exploitative fashion. The churchwardens and overseers could accumulate the wages of the poor while these unfortunates were underfed and overworked. Workhouses were often verminous and sources of disease, particularly gaol fever. At the Shoreditch workhouse near London it was discovered that thirty-nine children were sleeping in three beds.

Some parishes had poorhouses in which paupers could live rent-free. Others provided the poor a small amount of relief while permitting them to stay in their own cottages. One simply cannot generalize about the condition of the poor, for it would be different—sometimes very different—from parish to parish. People maintained in their own homes were said to receive "outdoor relief," those in workhouses or houses of correction, "indoor relief." The poor rates were collected from the propertied by the overseer of the poor of the parish.

Because of the degree of parish responsibility for the poor and its economic impact on the parishioners, persons with limited means found it very difficult to move from one parish and gain a settlement in another. In order to gain a settlement an individual had to meet one of four criteria: (1) pay taxes in the parish; (2) hold a public office in the parish; (3) serve an apprenticeship there; or (4) if unmarried, be hired for a year's service in the parish. However, with permission from two justices, a newcomer could be removed within 40 days if his dwelling had an annual value of less than £10 and if it appeared that he would become a burden to the parish. The person could not be removed, however, if he carried with him a proper certificate from the officers of his own parish. Another one of the ways in which the law of settlement was circumvented was the hiring of laborers for fifty-one weeks at a time; this was common and legal. The actual state of affairs is described precisely by J. L. Hammond and B. Hammond: "In real life, as in Fielding's pages, an obliging Justice, anxious to put an undesirable person out of the parish, would have had no difficulty in finding him guilty of some offence against the law, and such Justices were helped by the disreputable hangers-on who brought the legal profession into such bad odour" ("Poverty, Crime, Philanthropy," in Turberville, *Johnson's England,* 1:310).

Another snare faced by the poor was the system of vagrancy laws. The laws categorized offenders as (1) the disorderly, (2) rogues and vagabonds, and (3) incorrigible rogues. The "disorderly" included those who were idle and without employment, beggars, and anyone threatening to leave wife and children a burden upon the parish. Rogues and vagabonds included unlicensed pedlars and unauthorized strolling players. The vagrancy laws, obviously, could be interpreted in many ways and used punitively with little difficulty.

VIII. "Londoners"

In Johnson's time, as in our own, observers drew a distinction between what one might find in the capital and what one might find in the provinces. Then as now, however, human nature did not change at the borders of the city. Curiosities and perversities could be found virtually wherever they were sought. Yet the concentration of population within the city called attention to the actions, attitudes, and manners of the city's inhabitants. It is important for us to distinguish between those aspects of behavior which might appear in the city and those which one could find everywhere. The actions of the London mob, for example, might be duplicated elsewhere, but seldom with the force of numbers which the capital made possible. An interest in investments and finance would be found wherever there were people of means, but such interest would be concentrated in the city. The city might offer examples of extreme forms of behavior but one must hesitate before drawing causal lines between extremism and an urban address, particularly considering the fact that the wealthy often lived in the city for only a portion of the year, retiring to the countryside with the change of season or at the end of a parliamentary session.

My intention here is to discuss several aspects of London behavior which caught the attention of foreign visitors, but with the caveat that "London" behavior could be found in other places as well. What the foreigner found, however, would certainly be a part of the daily life of the capital, and while its importance could be exaggerated, the fact that Londoners were inured to certain types of behavior is instructive in itself.

The London crowd was brash and abusive; the ridicule of

Londoners walking through a private coach blocking their way.

passersby was one of its favorite pastimes. We misjudge the average eighteenth-century Londoner if we think of him as passive and subservient, knowing and enjoying his place within a hierarchic society. On the contrary, he was independent and assertive, although subject to political influences of a quite varied nature. Anecdotes abound concerning the Londoner and his exercise of individual liberty. For example, if the wealthy refused to move their coaches, the crowd would not hesitate to use the coaches as thoroughfares and walk right through them. Those who indulged in fashionable behavior were subject to the commentaries of the unappointed critic; there are several accounts, for example, of theatre-goers whose dress or hairstyles were so ridiculed by their fellows that they were forced to leave the premises.

Grosley noted that people in the street (day laborers, for example) were very rude to Frenchmen. In some cases the crowd moved from open insults to violent challenges. One

Englishman wearing French clothes was told that if he ever again entered the neighborhood in Parisian dress he would be thrown into the Thames (*A Tour to London*, 1:84, 87). Grosley's experience was that this sort of behavior was confined to the mob: "The politeness, the civility, and the officiousness of people of good breeding, whom we met in the streets, as well as the obliging readiness of the citizens and shopkeepers, even of the inferior sort, sufficiently indemnify and console us for the insolence of the mob; as I have often experienced" (ibid., p. 89). Moritz thought that anti-Semitism was stronger in England than in Germany (*Journeys of a German in England in 1782*, p. 105). Saussure traced certain forms of British behavior to another prejudice, one involving pride: "I do not think there is a people more prejudiced in its own favour than the British people, and they allow this to appear in their talk and manners. They look on foreigners in general with contempt, and think nothing is as well done elsewhere as in their own country" (*A Foreign View of England*, p. 177). Saussure also complains of rude and violent behavior on the part of the mob, particularly upon certain occasions, such as the Lord Mayor's Day:

> The populace on that day is particularly insolent and rowdy, turning into lawless freedom the great liberty it enjoys. At these times it is almost dangerous for an honest man, and more particularly for a foreigner, if at all well dressed, to walk in the streets, for he runs a great risk of being insulted by the vulgar populace, which is the most cursed brood in existence. He is sure of not only being jeered at and being bespattered with mud, but as likely as not dead dogs and cats will be thrown at him, for the mob makes a provision beforehand of these playthings, so that they may amuse themselves with them on the great day. [*A Foreign View of England*, pp. 111–12]

The hatred of foreigners was not confined to the London mob. In some cases in the provinces there was also a general antipathy toward strangers, including native Englishmen, some of whom were subjected to abuse by the suspicious. The villagers of Market Bosworth set their dogs on one man passing through for the simple reason that he was a stranger.

While the mob might be swayed by political demagogues of different ideological persuasions, its penchant for political fervor was not unique. As a people, the citizens of the eighteenth century were fiercely political, particularly those close to the center of political power in London. Archenholz comments on this phenomenon: "In general nothing is more difficult than to make an Englishman speak; he answers to every thing by *yes* or *no*; address him, however, on some political subject and he is suddenly animated; he opens his mouth and becomes eloquent; for this seems to be connected from his infancy with his very existence" (*A Picture of England*, p. 43). Addison's obsessively political upholsterer (*Tatler* 155) reappeared frequently in the period in slightly different literary form, but in every guise he was representative of the influence of politics on the individual Englishman. Such behavior was not confined to the world of literature. At a lord mayor's procession early in the century one foreign traveler saw three naked men running through the streets of London, vowing they would never wear coat or shirt until James II was restored to his throne (Bayne-Powell, *Travellers in Eighteenth-Century England*, p. 70). Politicization extended to nearly every area of life. For example, with the Methuen Treaty (1703) it was agreed that Portugal would allow the importation of English cloth. In return, England would lower the duty payable on Portuguese wine. The drinking of port became a favorite Whig activity, in part because it was prejudicial to French trade. The Jacobites, of course, turned to claret or burgundy.

Political activities, though sometimes silly, were not usually harmful. We have spoken already of numerous forms of violence and brutality in eighteenth-century life. The point is worth restating. The dangers of English life in the eighteenth century were everywhere. For example, Lord Holland's Eton fagmaster had forced him to toast bread in his bare hands, with the result that his fingers were permanently deformed. While the newspapers recorded acts of criminal violence (for exam-

Covent Garden Theatre riot, 1763.

ple, the case of Elizabeth Brownrigg, who was hanged in 1767 for torturing her apprentices to death, reported in detail in the *Annual Register*), much was simply taken for granted.

The theatre was a dangerous place. Moritz wrote of his experience at the Haymarket: "Every moment a rotten orange came whizzing past me or past my neighbour; one hit my hat, but I dared not turn round for fear one hit me in the face" (*Journeys of a German in England,* p. 61). Theatregoers came armed with rotten fruit and vegetables. They would probably not spend the 6d. for a theatre orange when one or two of them could be purchased outside for a halfpence. Poor Moritz was also a victim of vanity: "Behind me in the pit sat a young fop who continually put his foot on my bench in order to show off the flashy stone buckles on his shoes; if I didn't make way for his precious buckles he put his foot on my coat-tails" (ibid., p. 61).

A visitor to the House of Commons expecting decorous behavior and genteel debate was more likely to find constant

Londoners fleeing the city because of fear of earthquake.

milling about. Some would enter the room in spurs and sit cracking nuts or eating oranges while others attempted to speak. Gross and rough behavior were often the rule and not the exception. London, as Johnson noted, was not for the squeamish or the weak, and those who survived its challenges were likely to survive nearly anywhere else.

Some were not equal to its pressures and turned to suicide. Saussure reports that the property and land of suicides were confiscated and the suicides themselves buried at road crossings. He was shocked by the acceptance of the practice as well as the frequency of its occurrence: "I was much surprised at the light-hearted way in which men of this country commit suicide. I could not understand this mania, which astonished me as greatly as it does other foreigners" (*A Foreign View of England,* p. 201). In some cases stakes were driven through the suicides' hearts, presumably to prevent the individual's ghost from rising. This was foregone if it could be proven that the person was insane.

Grosley attributed English melancholy to fog, humidity, and

the smoke from coal fires, whose particles would "insinuate themselves into the blood of those who are always inhaling them, render it dull and heavy, and carry with them new principles of melancholy." His next comment is interesting: "Education, religion, public diversions, and the works of authors in vogue, seem to have no other end in view, but to feed and propagate this distemper" (*A Tour to London*, 1:167). Archenholz thought that most suicides resulted from Deism (*A Picture of England*, p. 111), but the English climate and the London atmosphere were more often cited as causes. The weather's oppressiveness is more commonly discussed than its extremes. There were exceptional occurrences, such as the earthquake of 1750, which left gaping holes in London streets and toppled chimneys. There were also extremes, such as the severe winter of 1784, in which the ground was covered with two feet of snow and evergreen trees froze and split. This was, however, far from normal: the snow which Kalm experienced was seldom on the ground for more than two or three days. The coal smoke, on the other hand, was nearly always present, as was the damp.

We think of the eighteenth century as enlightened, even though there is good reason (as Professor Pocock and others have argued) to avoid the use of the term "enlightenment" when speaking of English intellectual history. Yet, if we speak of social history, particularly among the uneducated, we realize the extent to which superstition remained a common part of experience. Many, for example, believed that a dead man's hands could cure warts if the hands were rubbed against them. The touch of men who had been hanged was sought for its effect in curing goiter and swollen glands. In the mid-seventies a woman in Leicestershire was thrown into a pond to see if she was a witch, the notion being that witches rejected baptism and hence the water would reject them. Suspected witches were bound foot to hand (actually thumb to toe) in criss-cross fashion before being tossed into the water. Usually a rope was tied to them to retrieve them if they demonstrated their innocence by sinking.

Suspected witches were sometimes weighed against the Bible; those found to be heavier were exonerated. In the seventeenth century it was not uncommon to encounter professional prickers, or witch finders. It was believed that a certain mark on the body indicated servitude to Satan. Satan, unfortunately, could be expected to hide the mark, and the mark would be insensitive. Thus, the suspected person was stripped and shaved of head and body hair; then any suspicious spots or marks were pricked with pins or sharp instruments. If no pain was apparent and no blood flowed when the pin was removed, it was assumed that the individual under examination was guilty. Although such practices were extremely rare in the eighteenth century, the last English witchcraft law was not repealed until 1736, and isolated examples of superstition and cruelty (such as the killing of a woman in Hertfordshire in 1751, reported in gory detail in the *Gentleman's Magazine*) still occurred.

While witches might not routinely be sought in the eighteenth century, the number of curious individuals a Londoner might encounter was potentially enormous. The Englishman has always prized his individuality and did so as much or more in the eighteenth century as in any other time. The eccentrics one meets in the pages of Fielding, Smollett, and Sterne had their counterparts in real life; Boswell (*Life,* 3:20–21) remarks on the great "variety of characters" Johnson had encountered. One sometimes has the impression that bizarre behavior was the rule and not the exception. Of course, it *was* exceptional, but it was in no way uncommon. One understates the case by saying that the period contained many colorful personalities, for the list of such persons is enormous, ranging from George Psalmanazar, whose phoney "Formosan" language was taught to would-be missionaries, to John Woodward, who would disrupt proceedings at Royal Society meetings by grimacing at those he disliked. "Characters" were everywhere and their continual emergence markedly contributed to the texture of daily life. The rich were particularly prone to acts of bravado, too. When the eccentric fourth Earl Ferrers was hanged (with a silken rope—a peer's privilege) for shooting his servant, he went to the gallows in his silver-braided wedding suit, noting

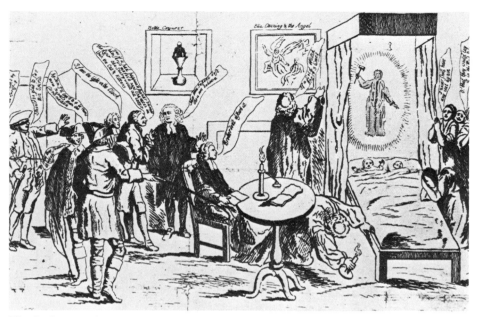

The Cock Lane "ghost."

that the day of his wedding and the day of his execution were the two worst in his life. Serving the rich could be a dangerous occupation in these days of sometimes strange opulence. Lord North, for example, was presented with a tiger as a gift from a sea captain; the tiger proceeded to bite a hand off of each of his two feeders.

Extremes of other sorts were often encountered and noted. An enormous farmer named Spooner, who weighed 40 stone and 9 pounds and was 4'3" across the shoulders was once stabbed at Atherstone market, but the knife did not penetrate all of the layers of fat on his body. In the 1770s a woman died at the age of 128; she had taken her third husband at the comparatively youthful age of 92.

Criminals and prostitutes were particularly known for great skill or brazen behavior. Jonathan Wild is said to have picked the parson's pocket before his execution, and we have already mentioned Mary Young, the pickpocket who equipped herself

Hogarth: Cunicularii, or the Wise Men of Godliman in Consultation (The Case of Mary Toft).

with artificial arms so that she could sit demurely in church while busily picking pockets. Kitty Fisher, the prostitute capable of commanding a fee of 100 guineas a night, is said to have boldly eaten a £1,000 banknote in a sandwich.

The period was one of great hoaxes. We have already noted George Psalmanazar's "Formosan" language. There was also the "ghost" in Cock Lane, which Johnson investigated (the ghost was reputed to be that of Lanny Lynes, which accused Lanny's lover, William Kent, of poisoning her) and the more bizarre case of Mary Toft, the woman who, it was claimed, gave birth to rabbits. Her case was investigated by George I's own physician, Nathanael St. André, who arrived on the scene just in time to "deliver" the trunk of a rabbit, an action which shattered his reputation. St. André described Mary Toft's rabbits as "praeter-natural."

The list of eccentricities and eccentrics is seemingly endless, from the Tahitian Omai, imported as a "noble savage" and lionized by London society, to Graham with his celestial bed and de Loutherbourg with his eidophusikon. Johnson's immersion in this world furnished an endless source of material for his curiosity and his fascination with human psychology and human behavior. It is a pity that he did not write more concerning the city, and we are, as has often been pointed out, deeply in Boswell's debt for the preservation of anecdotes, descriptions, and observations which would otherwise have passed into oblivion. Johnson's famous poem *London* is well worth considering in this connection. I have not discussed it up until now because its descriptive value is affected by its satiric intent, which leads Johnson to exaggerate certain of the city's ills in order to comment on politicians and political practices.

The poem has been criticized by scholarly commentators and not always for the right reasons. What is often overlooked is the fact that the poem has two narrators, only the second of which indulges in a lengthy jeremiad against the capital. The first speaker (the one who corresponds to the Juvenal figure in the poem Johnson is imitating) acknowledges the evils of the city:

Tho grief and fondness in my breast rebel,
When injur'd Thales bids the town farewell,
Yet still my calmer thoughts his choice commend,
I praise the hermit, but regret the friend,
Resolved at length, from vice and London far,
To breathe in distant fields a purer air,
And, fix'd on Cambria's solitary shore,
Give to St. David one true Briton more.
     For who would leave, unbrib'd, Hibernia's land,
Or change the rocks of Scotland for the Strand?
There none are swept by sudden fate away,
But all whom hunger spares, with age decay:
Here malice, rapine, accident, conspire,
And now a rabble rages, now a fire;
Their ambush here relentless ruffians lay,

And here the fell attorney prowls for prey;
Here falling houses thunder on your head,
And here a female atheist talks you dead.

It is sometimes argued that Thales represents Johnson's friend
the poet Richard Savage, though the dates will not permit such
an interpretation. (It may be, however, that Savage—a notorious poseur and posturer—imitated Thales.) Regardless of
Thales' identity, the Juvenalian parallel would suggest that the
first speaker corresponds to the poet himself—Johnson—and
that speaker remains in London at the poem's conclusion.
From all that we know of Johnson's experience and attitudes,
this is as it should be, for though he seldom distorted either the
city's good features or its bad, he remained a lover of the city
with all of its contrasts, contradictions, and extremes. Boswell
can sometimes stress the favorable aspects of Johnson's life in
the city; Johnson's *London* stresses the negative. The truth lies
in between.

The charges quoted in the segment from Johnson's *London*
are not exaggerated. One would easily find vice in Johnson's
London, and bad air and bribery would be omnipresent. Danger, disruption, street crime, fire, and the mob would not be
difficult to find either. There were predatory attorneys, lost
faith, and falling buildings also, but the counterbalancing features should be remembered: the felicity which Johnson found
in London taverns; the Strand's shops and the city's theatres;
the city's lights, its commercial vigor, and economic resilience;
the city's activity and power, its food and its fashions, its river
and its ships; its parks and shows, its papers and its personalities. Most of all there is its history and the network of associations one encounters in every section and at every corner.
Travelers then and now sometimes complain of the city, but
the occasions for complaint are dwarfed by the city's attractions. One sometimes hears the expression "only in London" as
a pained *cri de coeur,* but most often one hears it as an expression of joy.

Bibliography
Index

Bibliography

This bibliography is intended to provide a set of additional readings for those who wish to go beyond the introductory level of this book, but it is by no means exhaustive. The number of studies which treat eighteenth-century London and/or eighteenth-century life far exceeds the bounds and purposes of this bibliography. The interested reader should consult the bibliographies in many of the works here listed and browse in the appropriate locations in library stacks, realizing that the date of a given study is not a reliable guide to the extent of its usefulness. Some of the best books are old ones, particularly antiquarian books.

Adcock, A. St. John. *Famous Houses and Literary Shrines of London.* London: Dent, 1912.

Allen, Robert J. *The Clubs of Augustan London.* Cambridge: Harvard University Press, 1933.

Altick, Richard D. *The Shows of London.* Cambridge: Harvard University Press, 1978.

Archenholz, Johann Wilhelm, baron von. *A Picture of England, Containing a Description of the Laws, Customs, and Manners of England.* Dublin, 1791.

Arnold, Janet. *Perukes and Periwigs.* London: H. M. Stationery Office, 1970.

Ashe, Geoffrey. *Do What You Will: A History of Anti-Morality.* London: W. H. Allen, 1974.

Ashton, John. *Social Life in the Reign of Queen Anne Taken from Original Sources.* New York: Scribner's, 1929.

Atherton, Herbert M. *Political Prints in the Age of Hogarth: A Study of the Ideographic Representation of Politics.* Oxford: Clarendon, 1974.

Barber, Giles. "Dr. Johnson and Cookery." In *The Dress of Words: Essays on Restoration and Eighteenth-Century Literature in Honor of Richmond P. Bond,* ed. Robert B. White, Jr. Lawrence: University of Kansas Libraries, 1978.

Barrell, John. *The Dark Side of the Landscape: The Rural Poor in English Painting, 1730–1840.* Cambridge: Cambridge University Press, 1980.

Bate, W. Jackson. *Samuel Johnson.* New York: Harcourt Brace Jovanovich, 1977.

Bayne-Powell, Rosamond. *The English Child in the Eighteenth Century.* London: John Murray, 1939.

Bayne-Powell, Rosamond. *Housekeeping in the Eighteenth Century.* London: John Murray, 1956.

Bayne-Powell, Rosamond. *Travellers in Eighteenth-Century England.* London: John Murray, 1951.

Bell, Walter George. *Fleet Street in Seven Centuries.* London: Pitman, 1912.

Berry, George. *Taverns and Tokens of Pepys' London.* London: Seaby, 1978.

Bloom, Edward A. *Samuel Johnson in Grub Street.* Providence: Brown University Press, 1957.

Bond, Donald F., ed. *The Spectator.* 5 vols. Oxford: Clarendon, 1965.

Borer, Mary Cathcart. *People of Georgian England.* London: Macdonald, 1969.

Boswell, James. *Boswell for the Defence, 1769–1774.* Ed. William K. Wimsatt, Jr., and Frederick A. Pottle. New York: McGraw-Hill, 1959.

Boswell, James. *Boswell's Journal of a Tour to the Hebrides with Samuel Johnson, LL.D.* Ed. Frederick A. Pottle and Charles H. Bennett. 2nd ed. New York: McGraw-Hill, 1961.

Boswell, James. *Boswell's Life of Johnson.* Ed. G. B. Hill; rev. and enlarged by L. F. Powell. 6 vols. Oxford: Clarendon, 1934–50.

Boswell, James. *Boswell's London Journal, 1762–1763.* Ed. Frederick A. Pottle. New York: McGraw-Hill, 1950.

Boswell, James. *Boswell on the Grand Tour: Germany and Switzerland, 1764.* Ed. Frederick A. Pottle. New York: McGraw-Hill, 1953.

Boswell, James. *Boswell on the Grand Tour: Italy, Corsica, and France, 1765–1766.* Ed. Frank Brady and Frederick A. Pottle. New York: McGraw-Hill, 1955.

Brander, Michael. *The Georgian Gentleman.* Farnborough, Hants.: Saxon House, 1973.

Brown, Ivor. *Dr. Johnson and His World.* London: Lutterworth Press, 1965.

Brown, Ivor. *London: An Illustrated History.* London: London House and Maxwell, 1966.

Buer, M. C. *Health, Wealth, and Population in the Early Days of the Industrial Revolution*. London: Routledge, 1926.

Burnett, John. *A History of the Cost of Living*. Harmondsworth: Penguin, 1969.

Burton, Elizabeth. *The Georgians at Home, 1714–1830*. London: Longmans, 1967.

Campbell, Thomas. *Dr. [Thomas] Campbell's Diary of a Visit to England in 1775*. Ed. James L. Clifford. Cambridge: Cambridge University Press, 1947.

Carrier, Robert, and Oliver Lawson Dick. *The Vanished City: A Study of London*. London: Hutchinson, 1957.

Chancellor, E. Beresford. *The Eighteenth Century in London: An Account of Its Social Life and Arts*. London: Batsford, n.d.

Clifford, James L. *Dictionary Johnson: Samuel Johnson's Middle Years*. New York: McGraw-Hill, 1979.

Clifford, James L. "Some Aspects of London Life in the Mid-Eighteenth Century." In *City and Society in the Eighteenth Century*, ed. Paul Fritz and David Williams. Toronto: Hakkert, 1973.

Cockburn, J. S., ed. *Crime in England, 1550–1800*. Princeton: Princeton University Press, 1977.

Cragg, Gerald R. *The Church and the Age of Reason, 1648–1789*. Harmondsworth: Penguin, 1960.

Cunnington, C. Willett, and Phillis Cunnington. *Handbook of English Costume in the Eighteenth Century*. London: Faber and Faber, 1957.

Cunnington, C. Willett, and Phillis Cunnington. *The History of Underclothes*. London: Michael Joseph, 1951.

Curley, Thomas M. *Samuel Johnson and the Age of Travel*. Athens: University of Georgia Press, 1976.

Curtis, Lewis P., and Herman W. Liebert. *Esto Perpetua: The Club of Dr. Johnson and His Friends, 1764–1784*. Hamden: Archon Books, 1963.

Darlington, Ida, and James Howgego. *Printed Maps of London circa 1553–1850*. London: George Philip and Son, 1964.

Defoe, Daniel. *The Complete English Tradesman*. 2 vols. London, 1726–27.

Defoe, Daniel. *A Journal of the Plague Year*. Ed. Anthony Burgess and Christopher Bristow. Harmondsworth: Penguin, 1966.

Defoe, Daniel. *A Tour Thro' the whole Island of Great Britain*. 3 vols. London, 1724–27.

Dobson, Austin. "Johnson's Houses." *Illustrated London News*, March 10, 1894, p. 295.

Dobson, Austin. *Side-walk Studies*. London: Chatto and Windus, 1902.

Drummond, J. C., and Anne Wilbraham. *The Englishman's Food: A History of Five Centuries of English Diet*. Rev. ed. London: Jonathan Cape, 1958.

Earle, Peter. *The World of Defoe*. New York: Atheneum, 1977.

Ede, Mary. *Arts and Society in England under William and Mary*. London: Stainer and Bell, 1979.

Eden, Sir Frederic Morton. *The State of the Poor: A History of the Labouring Classes in England*. 3 vols. London, 1797.

Evelyn, John. *The Diary of John Evelyn*. Ed. E. S. de Beer. London: Oxford University Press, 1959.

Fielding, Henry. *An Enquiry into the Causes of the late Increase of Robbers, &c. with some Proposals for Remedying this Growing Evil*. London, 1751.

Fisher, Allan C., Jr. " 'The City': London's Storied Square Mile." *National Geographic* 119 (June 1961): 735–77.

Foucault, Michel. *Madness and Civilization: A History of Insanity in the Age of Reason*. Trans. Richard Howard. New York: Mentor, 1967.

Fraser, Antonia. *A History of Toys*. New York: Delacorte, 1966.

Gay, John. *Trivia; or, The Art of Walking the Streets of London*. Ed. W. H. Williams. London: Daniel O'Connor, 1922.

George, M. Dorothy. *England in Johnson's Day*. London: Methuen, 1928.

George, M. Dorothy. *England in Transition: Life and Work in the Eighteenth Century*. Harmondsworth: Penguin, 1962.

George, M. Dorothy. *London Life in the Eighteenth Century*. New York: Harper and Row, 1965.

Gloag, John. *A Short Dictionary of Furniture*. New York: Holt, Rinehart and Winston, 1965.

Goldgar, Bertrand A. *Walpole and the Wits: The Relation of Politics to Literature, 1722–1742*. Lincoln: University of Nebraska Press, 1976.

Gorely, Jean. *Wedgwood*. New York: Gramercy, 1950.

Grant, Douglas. *The Cock Lane Ghost*. London: Macmillan, 1965.

Gray, Ernest, "ed." *The Diary of a Surgeon in the Year 1751–1752 by John Knyveton*. . . . New York: Appleton Century, 1937.

Greene, Donald J. *Samuel Johnson's Library: An Annotated Guide*. English Literary Studies, University of Victoria, vol. 1. Victoria, B.C., 1975.

Grosley, Peter-John. *A Tour to London; or, New Observations on England and Its Inhabitants*. Trans. Thomas Nugent. 2 vols. London, 1772.

Hagstrum, Jean H. *Sex and Sensibility: Ideal and Erotic Love from Milton to Mozart*. Chicago: University of Chicago Press, 1980.

Hair, Paul, ed. *Before the Bawdy Court*. London: Elek, 1972.

Halliday, F. E. *Doctor Johnson and His World*. London: Thames and Hudson, 1968.

Halls, Zillah. *Men's Costume, 1750–1800*. London: H. M. Stationery Office, 1973.

Halls, Zillah. *Women's Costume, 1600–1750*. London: H. M. Stationery Office, 1970.

Hampden, John. *An Eighteenth-Century Journal: Being a Record of the Years 1774–1776*. London: Macmillan, 1940.

Harmsworth, Cecil, Lord. *Dr. Johnson's House, Gough Square*. Rev. ed. London: Trustees of Dr. Johnson's House, 1977.

Hart, Roger. *English Life in the Eighteenth Century*. London: Wayland, 1970.

Hartmann, Cyril Hughes, ed. *Games and Gamesters of the Restoration*. Port Washington, N.Y.: Kennikat, 1971. Includes Cotton, *The Compleat Gamester*, and Lucas, *Lives of the Gamesters*.

Hawkins, Sir John. *The Life of Samuel Johnson, LL.D.* 2nd ed. London, 1787.

Hay, Douglas, et al. *Albion's Fatal Tree: Crime and Society in Eighteenth-Century England*. New York: Pantheon, 1975.

Hayes, John. *London: A Pictorial History*. London: Batsford, 1969.

Hill, Douglas. *A Hundred Years of Georgian London, from the Accession of George I to the Heyday of the Regency*. London: Macdonald, 1970.

Himes, Norman E. *Medical History of Contraception*. New York: Gamut Press, 1963.

Hole, Christina. *A Mirror of Witchcraft*. London: Chatto and Windus, 1957.

Holloway, John, and Joan Black, eds. *Later England Broadside Ballads*. London: University of Nebraska Press, 1975.

Holmes, Ronald. *Witchcraft in British History*. London: Frederick Muller, 1974.

Howard, John. *The State of the Prisons in England and Wales, with Preliminary Observations, and an Account of some Foreign Prisons*. Warrington, 1777. *Appendix*, 1780.

Humphreys, A. R. *The Augustan World: Society, Thought, and Letters in Eighteenth-Century England*. London: Methuen, 1954.

Hyde, Mary. *The Thrales of Streatham Park*. Cambridge: Harvard University Press, 1977.

Jacob, Margaret C. *The Newtonians and the English Revolution, 1689–1720*. Ithaca: Cornell University Press, 1976.

James, Robert. *A Medicinal Dictionary. . . .* 3 vols. London, 1743–45.

Jarrett, Derek. *England in the Age of Hogarth*. New York: Viking, 1974.

Johnson, Samuel. *Diaries, Prayers, and Annals*. Ed. E. L. McAdam, Jr., with Donald Hyde and Mary Hyde. New Haven: Yale University Press, 1958.

Johnson, Samuel. *A Dictionary of the English Language*. Introduction by James L. Clifford. 2 vols. Beirut: Librairie du Liban, 1978.

Johnson, Samuel. *The Idler and the Adventurer*. Ed. W. J. Bate, John M. Bullitt, and L. F. Powell. New Haven: Yale University Press, 1963.

Johnson, Samuel. *A Journey to the Western Islands of Scotland*. Ed. Mary Lascelles. New Haven: Yale University Press, 1971.

Johnson, Samuel. *The Letters of Samuel Johnson: With Mrs. Thrale's Genuine Letters to Him*. Ed. R. W. Chapman. 3 vols. Oxford: Clarendon, 1952.

Johnson, Samuel. *Life of Savage*. Ed. Clarence Tracy. Oxford: Clarendon, 1971.

Johnson, Samuel. *Poems*. Ed. E. L. McAdam, Jr., with George Milne. New Haven: Yale University Press, 1964.

Johnson, Samuel. *The Rambler*. Ed. W. J. Bate and Albrecht B. Strauss. 3 vols. New Haven: Yale University Press, 1969.

Johnson, Samuel. *The Works of Samuel Johnson, LL.D.* 9 vols. Oxford, 1825.

Jones, Louis C. *The Clubs of the Georgian Rakes*. New York: Columbia University Press, 1942.

Kalm, Pehr. *Kalm's Account of His Visit to England on His Way to America in 1748*. Trans. Joseph Lucas. London: Macmillan, 1892.

Kielmansegge, Count Frederick. *Diary of a Journey to England in the Years 1761–1762*. Trans. Countess Kielmansegg [*sic*]. London: Longmans, Green, 1902.

Kronenberger, Louis. *Kings and Desperate Men: Life in Eighteenth-Century England*. New York: Knopf, 1942.

Landa, Louis A. "London Observed: The Progress of a Simile." *From Chaucer to Gibbon, Essays in Memory of Curt A. Zimansky, Philological Quarterly* #54 (1975): 275–88.

Lane, Margaret. *Samuel Johnson and His World*. London: Hamish Hamilton, 1976.

La Rochefoucauld. *A Frenchman in England, 1784, Being the "Mélanges sur L'Angleterre" of François de la Rochefoucauld*. Ed. Jean Marchand; trans. S. C. Roberts. Cambridge: Cambridge University Press, 1933.

Lewis, Wilmarth Sheldon. *Three Tours through London in the Years 1748–1776–1797*. New Haven: Yale University Press, 1941.

Liebert, Herman W. "Portraits of the Author: Lifetime Likenesses of Samuel Johnson." In *English Portraits of the Seventeenth and Eighteenth Centuries*. Los Angeles: William Andrews Clark Memorial Library, UCLA, 1974.

McConnell, Frank. *Storytelling and Mythmaking: Images from Film and*

Literature. New York: Oxford University Press, 1979.

MacKinnon, F. D. "Dr. Johnson and the Temple." *Cornhill Magazine* 57 (October 1924): 465–77.

Maclean, Virginia. *Much Entertainment: A Visual and Culinary Record of Johnson and Boswell's Tour of Scotland in 1773.* London: Dent, 1973.

Malcolmson, Robert W. *Popular Recreations in English Society, 1700–1850.* Cambridge: Cambridge University Press, 1973.

Mannix, Daniel P. *The Hell Fire Club.* New York: Ballantine, 1959.

Maré, Eric de. *London's River: The Story of a City.* New York: McGraw-Hill, 1965.

Marshall, Dorothy. *Eighteenth-Century England.* New York: McKay, 1962.

Marshall, Dorothy. *English People in the Eighteenth Century.* London: Longmans, 1956.

Marshall, Dorothy. *The English Poor in the Eighteenth Century: A Study in Social and Administrative History.* London: Routledge and Kegan Paul, 1926.

Mingay, G. E. *Georgian London.* London: Batsford, 1975.

Moritz, Carl Philip. *Journeys of a German in England in 1782.* Ed. and trans. Reginald Nettel. New York: Holt, Rinehart and Winston, 1965.

Morris, Richard. *Cathedrals and Abbeys of England and Wales: The Building Church, 600–1540.* New York: Norton, 1979.

The New Newgate Calendar; or, Malefactor's Bloody Register. 5 vols. London, 1773.

Newton, A. Edward. *The Greatest Book in the World and Other Papers.* Boston: Little, Brown, 1925.

Nicoll, Allardyce. *The Garrick Stage: Theatres and Audience in the Eighteenth Century.* Ed. Sybil Rosenfeld. Athens: University of Georgia Press, 1980.

Parreaux, André. *Daily Life in England in the Reign of George III.* Trans. Carola Congreve. London: George Allen and Unwin, 1969.

Paston, George [E. M. Symonds]. *Social Caricature in the Eighteenth Century.* London: Methuen, 1905.

Paulson, Ronald *Hogarth: His Life, Art, and Times.* 2 vols. New Haven: Yale University Press, 1971.

Pennant, Thomas. *Some Account of London.* 2nd ed. London, 1791.

Phillips, Hugh. *Mid-Georgian London: A Topographical and Social Survey of Central and Western London about 1750.* London: Collins, 1964.

Phillips, Hugh. *The Thames about 1750.* London: Collins, 1951.

Piozzi, Hester Lynch Thrale. *Anecdotes of the Late Samuel Johnson, LL.D.*

In *Johnsonian Miscellanies,* ed. G. B. Hill, vol. 1. Oxford: Clarendon, 1897.

Plumb, J. H. *The Commercialisation of Leisure in Eighteenth-Century England.* Reading: University of Reading, 1973.

Plumb, J. H. *England in the Eighteenth Century.* Harmondsworth: Penguin, 1950.

Pocock, J.G.A. "Post-Puritan England and the Problem of the Enlightenment." In *Culture and Politics from Puritanism to the Enlightenment,* ed. Perez Zagorin. Berkeley and Los Angeles: University of California Press, 1980.

Quennell, Marjorie, and C.H.B. Quennell. *A History of Everyday Things in England.* Vol. 3, *1733 to 1851.* 6th ed. London: Batsford, 1961.

Quinlan, Maurice J. *Victorian Prelude: A History of English Manners, 1700–1830.* New York: Columbia University Press, 1941.

Radzinowicz, Leon. *A History of English Criminal Law and Its Administration from 1750.* 4 vols. New York: Macmillan, 1948–68.

Reddaway, T. F. *The Rebuilding of London after the Great Fire.* London: Jonathan Cape, 1940.

Richardson, John. *Covent Garden.* New Barnet: Historical Publications, 1979.

Riely, John. "The Hours of the Georgian Day." *History Today* 24 (May 1974): 307–14.

Rocque, John. *A Plan of the Cities of London and Westminster, and Borough of Southwark; with the Contiguous Buildings.* London, 1746. (Reprint, ed. Harry Margary, with an introduction by James Howgego. Lympne Castle, Kent: Harry Margary; and Chichester: Phillimore and Co., 1971.

Rudé, George. *Hanoverian London, 1714–1808.* Berkeley and Los Angeles: University of California Press, 1971.

Saussure, César de. *A Foreign View of England in the Reigns of George I. and George II.: The Letters of Monsieur César de Saussure to his Family.* Trans. Madame von Muyden. New York: Dutton, 1902.

Sedgwick, Romney, ed. *Lord Hervey's Memoirs.* London: William Kimber, 1952.

Shryock, Richard Harrison. *The Development of Modern Medicine: An Interpretation of the Social and Scientific Factors Involved.* Madison: University of Wisconsin Press, 1979.

Smith, Al. *Dictionary of City of London Street Names.* Newton Abbot: David and Charles, 1970.

Smith, E. *The Compleat Housewife; or, Accomplish'd Gentlewoman's Com-*

panion. London, 1753. (Reprint, London: Literary Services and Production, 1968.

Smollett, Tobias. *Humphry Clinker.* Ed. Lewis M. Knapp. London: Oxford University Press, 1966.

Stone, Lawrence. *The Family, Sex, and Marriage in England, 1500–1800.* New York: Harper and Row, 1977.

Strutt, Joseph. *The Sports and Pastimes of the People of England.* London, 1830.

Summerson, John. *Georgian London.* London: Pleiades, 1945.

Taylor, Duncan. *Fielding's England.* London: Dennis Dobson, 1966.

Thompson, E. P. *Whigs and Hunters: The Origin of the Black Act.* New York: Pantheon, 1975.

Thompson, Roger. *Unfit for Modest Ears: A Study of Pornographic, Obscene, and Bawdy Works Written or Published in England in the Second Half of the Seventeenth Century.* Totowa, N.J.: Rowman and Littlefield, 1979.

Tinker, Chauncey Brewster. *Dr. Johnson and Fanny Burney: Being the Johnsonian Passages from the Works of Mme. d'Arblay.* New York: Moffat, Yard and Co., 1911.

Tinker, Chauncey Brewster. *The Salon and English Letters: Chapters on the Interrelations of Literature and Society in the Age of Johnson.* New York: Macmillan, 1915.

Todd, Dennis. "Three Characters in Hogarth's *Cunicularii*—and Some Implications." *Eighteenth-Century Studies* 16 (Fall 1982): 26–46.

Trevelyan, G. M. *Illustrated English Social History.* Vol. 3. London: Longmans, 1951.

Turberville, A. S. *English Men and Manners in the Eighteenth Century.* New York: Oxford University Press, 1957.

Turberville, A. S., ed. *Johnson's England: An Account of the Life and Manners of His Age.* 2 vols. Oxford: Clarendon, 1933.

Voltaire, François-Marie Arouet de. *Philosophical Letters.* Trans. Ernest Dilworth. Indianapolis: Bobbs-Merrill, 1961.

Ward. C. A. "London Homes of Dr. Johnson." *The Antiquary* 17 (January–February 1888): 12–15, 53–55.

Wright, Lawrence. *Clean and Decent: The Fascinating History of the Bathroom and the Water Closet.* London: Routledge and Kegan Paul, 1960.

Zagorin, Perez, ed. *Culture and Politics from Puritanism to the Enlightenment.* Berkeley and Los Angeles: University of California Press, 1980.

Zupko, Ronald Edward. *British Weights and Measures: A History from Antiquity to the Seventeenth Century.* Madison: University of Wisconsin Press, 1977.

Zupko, Ronald Edward. *A Dictionary of English Weights and Measures from Anglo-Saxon Times to the Nineteenth Century.* Madison: University of Wisconsin Press, 1968.

Index